SOFTWARE TESTING EXPLAINED

A COMPREHENSIVE GUIDE FOR IT AND NON-IT
PROFESSIONALS TO THRIVE IN A HIGH-DEMAND
FIELD, DRIVE BUSINESS VALUE, BOOST EFFICIENCY,
AND MAXIMIZE SAVINGS FOR BIG CORPORATIONS

JAIME MANTILLA, MSIT

CONTENTS

This book is dedicated to my wife, my children, my sister, my parents, and everyone that has been part of my career development and has been a coach and/or mentor throughout my journey.

INTRODUCTION

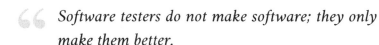 *Software testers do not make software; they only make them better.*

— ANONYMOUS

Whenever you are using software, have you ever stopped to think about all the processes that it goes through before you can use it with minimum problems? This is because after the developers write the code that creates it, it goes through several tests that are carried out by professionals dedicated to this task. These individuals are known as **software testers**, and their job is to ensure that what is being released to the user is mostly free of errors (bugs or defects), safe, and functional.

Even if you have heard about these professionals before, or maybe even this process, I can imagine that the first thing that comes to mind is someone who randomly clicks at buttons and features to make sure they are working. If it is, don't worry—you are not the only one. Several people have this perception, and it is because what software testers do is something so complex and filled with procedures that even some professionals in the market don't completely know what it entails.

Software testing has several nuances, and there are several different types that can be carried out, as I will show you in this book. While the process may take some time, if a program is not properly tested, it has the potential to incur financial losses for the company or the individual that uses it. Since most of the companies are built on technology and use it to operate, you might imagine the problem it can be if there is a fault in them.

If you think about it, if bank software is not tested, it might lead to customers being unable to access their money and make payments. Patients in hospitals depend on programs to have access to their medication and status monitoring. Even the simplest things, such as the application that you use to watch your favorite series, need to be tested to ensure that you have the correct recommendation according to your preferences.

As you have seen, a software tester is as important as the developer throughout the process of delivering a program to the public. Companies that want to ensure that their product is secure and that it delivers quality must employ these professionals to guarantee that the risks of failure are as reduced as possible.

Therefore, one should consider quality assurance and software testing a **must** within their corporate IT strategy. By seeing the process as an essential step of the process and not an additional expense, you will actually end up **saving** money and keeping your information safe. It will also bring more customer satisfaction and structure the process of software development—from the gathering of requisites to the final delivery.

In this book, I will speak about two categories of software testing: functional and non-functional. As you will see, each of these has its own characteristics and approach to validating the functioning of a program. The other category, maintenance testing, will not be approached because the tests that comprise it are almost the same as those that you will use in the other two.

Nevertheless, the content I provide in this book gives you a general but deep understanding of how to approach software testing. With the information here, which I have gathered throughout my professional experience, you will see processes that some people take years to learn and understand. My main objective is to give you a complete guide to help you feel confident enough to decide to move forward.

ABOUT THE AUTHOR

My name is Jaime Mantilla, and I came to the United States from Colombia with my family when I was 17 years old. I had no friends and didn't speak English; the only thing that motivated me was fulfilling the American dream.

I started working as a janitor for $5.25/hour not keeping one dime of what I made. Everything I earned was given to my parents to provide for our family. It took me around one year to start speaking English comfortably and get everything in place to start getting other jobs to work my way up.

Until I was able to establish myself, I worked a bunch of jobs—from selling knives to making and delivering pizza, as well as delivering auto parts and as a cook in a Mediterranean restaurant. Some of the jobs were normal, such as being a waiter, and others were a little more unusual, such as serving for a nudist colony. Everything was worth the effort of making my dreams come true and providing for my family.

And all the work paid off. Today, I am an IT professional who has been working in the area for more than 12 years. I obtained my Bachelor's degree in Management Information Systems and have the title of Master of Science in Information Technology. In addition to this, I hold several certifications in the area, all of which have enabled me to work for multiple Inc 500 companies in the most varied industries. Some of these include Citibank, Price Waterhouse Cooper, Raymond James Financial, Suddath, Cigna, and ALSAC, where I worked with software and automation engineering.

Today I am an IT consultant and entrepreneur, happily married, with two kids. I decided to write this book because of my life and professional experience, knowledge, and passion for the topic. My main objective is to help others strive in their personal and professional careers, and show the versatile options that entering the software testing industry entails.

To me, helping you understand software testing in the software development life cycle matters deeply. And there are two main reasons for this. The first is that everyone should know the importance and the impact on organizations that this process has. Although it might seem irrelevant, you will see, by reading this book, that it helps save money throughout the development process, as well as protect your information and avoid any problems once the software is launched. If you are a manager in the company you work for, this might bring you a few solutions once you understand how the process is developed and the benefits that applying it will bring.

The second reason is because what you're about to learn can help you land your dream job and improve your life. This book will enable you to speak confidently about the topic, helping you drive business and technical conversations with others in the market. Maybe, at the end, once you have a full grasp of what this activity entails, you will become as passionate as I am about the industry and consider applying for it.

The information you will obtain from this book—whether you are an IT professional or not—will help you understand each of the phases of the process. In addition to this, the knowledge you will gain will enable you to start your journey into software testing, if that is something you wish to do. I hope you have a good read, and I'll see you at the end!

1

AN INTRODUCTION TO
SOFTWARE TESTING

> *The problem is not that testing is the bottleneck. The problem is that you don't know what's in the bottle. That's a problem that testing addresses.*

> — MICHAEL BOLTON

Before we dive into the important techniques and terms that software testing entails, it is important to understand what software testing is actually about, why it is so important, and why it is a great idea to get into the software testing industry.

WHAT IS SOFTWARE TESTING AND HOW DOES IT WORK?

Software testing is the process of evaluating software or systems to identify defects and issues before they are released to end users. The goal of testing is to ensure that the software meets the specified requirements and performs as expected. In addition to this, another important aspect of software testing is the financial and strategic advantages it brings to companies that are developing new software. When you consider that if a bug in software reaches the public or if there is a security breach, this could lead to serious reputational issues for the company, leading to a loss in revenue. Therefore, considering software testing as part of the plan when you intend to develop a new program is essential.

For people who want to enter the area of software testing, it is important to understand the different types of testing that are used, such as functional testing, regression testing, performance testing, and security testing (*Types of Software Testing: Different Testing Types with Details*, 2023). Functional testing involves testing the software to ensure that it performs the intended functions correctly, while regression testing involves testing the software after changes have been made to ensure that existing functionality has not been negatively affected. Performance testing involves testing the software's ability to handle large amounts of data and traffic, while security testing involves testing the software's ability to protect against unauthorized access and other security threats.

If you are already in the area of software testing, it is important to stay up-to-date with the latest tools and techniques for your activity, such as test automation, continuous integration, and agile testing (*Types of Software Testing: Different Testing Types with Details*, 2023). Test automation involves using software tools to automate the testing process, making it faster and more efficient. Continuous integration involves regularly testing the software as changes are made, to ensure that any defects or issues are identified and fixed as soon as possible. Agile testing involves incorporating testing into the agile development process to ensure that testing is done throughout the development cycle.

The importance of software testing cannot be overstated. Testing helps reduce the costs of development by identifying defects and issues early in the process before they become more difficult and expensive to fix. Testing also helps to improve the quality of the software or system, making it more reliable and user-friendly. By ensuring that software is thoroughly tested before it is released, stakeholders can avoid costly and embarrassing bugs and defects that can damage their reputation and lead to a loss of revenue (Mosconi, 2022).

Essentially speaking, we can say that testing is an essential part of the software development process, and it is important for people who want to enter and for those who are already in the area to understand its importance and how it works. By using the latest tools and techniques for testing software and incorporating testing into the agile development process, developers can reduce costs, improve quality, and ensure that their software is reliable and user-friendly.

Although we have already mentioned some of the software testing techniques, I want to mention a few more. However, I say a few more because, toward the end of the book, we will have a comprehensive look at all the testing that can be performed with examples and their importance. For now, let's take a look at some of the most common test types and what they do.

Types of Software Testing

There are several types of software testing that are used to ensure software quality. As I mentioned earlier, in this section we will discuss the most important types of software testing and their significance in reducing costs and improving software quality. However, I want to once again reiterate that these are not the only types of testing and that we will take a further look at them in Chapters 5 and 6 of this book. You must first consider that testing software can be either a manual or an automated process that will depend on the characteristics of each company and the needs that the program requires. Here are eight of the most popular forms of software testing:

1. **Functional testing**: Functional testing is also known as **component testing** and is a type of testing that ensures that the software meets the functional requirements of the system. It involves testing the software functions against the specified requirements and verifying that they perform as expected. The main objective of functional testing is to ensure that the software does what it is supposed to do.

2. **Regression testing**: Regression testing is used to ensure that the changes made to the software do not have any unintended effects on the existing functionalities. It involves retesting the software after making modifications to the code, and it verifies that the software still

behaves as expected after the changes are made.

3. **Performance testing**: Performance testing is used to evaluate the software's ability to handle a high load by simulating the actual usage conditions of the software. It tests the software's **speed**, **scalability**, and **stability** under various load conditions. Performance testing is crucial to ensure that the software can handle the expected load and provide the desired user experience.

4. **Security testing**: Security testing is an essential type of software testing that assesses the software's ability to protect against unauthorized access, data theft, or other security threats. It involves testing the software against different types of security vulnerabilities, such as buffer overflows, SQL injection, cross-site scripting, and other attacks.

5. **Usability testing**: Usability testing is another important type of software testing that is conducted to evaluate the software's ease of use and its user-friendliness. It involves testing the software against usability standards and user needs and verifying that it provides an intuitive and efficient user experience.

6. **Compatibility testing**: Compatibility testing is used to ensure that the software works seamlessly across different operating systems, devices, and browsers. It involves testing the software against different platforms and configurations and verifying that it functions as expected.

7. **Acceptance testing**: Acceptance testing is a type of testing that is conducted to validate the software against the user's acceptance criteria. It involves testing the software against the user's requirements and verifying that it meets the expected standards and specifications.

8. **Exploratory testing**: Exploratory testing is a type of testing that involves exploring the software's functionalities to identify defects that may not be captured by other types of testing. It involves testing the software in an unstructured and ad-hoc manner, and it helps uncover defects that may be missed by other testing methods.

Software testing is an essential part of the software development process that helps reduce costs by catching defects early in the development cycle. By using a variety of testing techniques, developers can ensure that their software is reliable, efficient, and user-friendly.

History of Software Testing

The history of software testing dates back to the early days of computing, when software programs were manually tested by developers to ensure that they were functioning as intended. However, as software applications became more complex, the need for more formalized testing procedures became increasingly important.

One of the earliest recorded instances of software testing occurred in 1949, when the Harvard Mark II computer crashed due to a software bug (Hernandez, 2020). This incident led to the development of the first bug-tracking system, which was used to identify and fix defects in software programs.

Fun fact! This first "bug" that I mentioned, believe it or not, was actually a real bug—a moth (Whyman, n.d.)! Even though the moth was a bug interfering with the hardware that made it have trouble working, the term "bug" comes from before that, actually in the 1800s. The label was first applied by Thomas Edison in a letter where he talked about issues he found with the telephone.

Let's take a look at software testing through the decades:

- **1960s**: Software testing began to gain more prominence as software applications became more complex and were used in a wider range of industries. During this time, structured testing methodologies were developed, which helped to formalize the testing process and make it more efficient.
- **1970s**: As software systems became increasingly complex, the need for more advanced testing methods grew. The concept of structured testing was introduced, which emphasized the importance of a systematic approach to software testing. This approach involved creating test cases based on the various functions and features of the software and then systematically testing each case to ensure that the software was functioning properly.
- **1980s**: Software testing continued to evolve with the introduction of object-oriented programming and the development of new testing techniques such as white box testing and black box testing.

- **1990s**: The concept of test-driven development (TDD) was introduced, which involved writing automated tests before the code was written.

In addition to this, it is important to note that in the 1970s and 1980s, automated testing tools began to emerge, which helped speed up the testing process and make it more reliable. During this time, the concept of quality assurance (QA) also emerged, which helped to ensure that software applications met certain standards and specifications.

Today, software testing has become an essential part of the software development lifecycle, and there are a wide range of testing methodologies and tools available to help ensure that applications are reliable, robust, and efficient. Software testing is a critical component of the software development lifecycle, and there is a wide range of testing tools and methodologies available to developers. You have already seen some of the benefits that software testing brings to the organization, but maybe we should take a closer look to see if we can identify any others. Read on to find out!

SOFTWARE TESTING EXPLAINED | 27

WHAT ARE THE BENEFITS OF SOFTWARE TESTING?

The benefits of software testing are numerous and can be very valuable for both those who are new to the field and those who are already working in it. One of the main ones? You got it right! Saving money. Since companies work and exist for the purposes of generating revenue, saving money can be considered the most important of this service's features.

One of the reasons why is that when you incorporate software testing into the development strategy, it helps in identifying defects and errors in the early stages of the software life cycle. This helps reduce the cost of fixing defects, as it is much cheaper to fix defects in the early stages of development than in the later stages. According to a study by IBM (2019), the cost of fixing a defect in the production phase is about four to five times higher than fixing it in the requirements phase. Here are a few other cases presented by IBM (2019):

> Consider Nissan having to recall over 1 million cars due to a software defect in the airbag sensor detectors. Or a software bug that caused the failure of a USD 1.2 billion military satellite launch. The numbers speak for themselves. Software failures in the US cost the economy

USD 1.1 trillion in assets in 2016. What's more, they impacted 4.4 billion customers (*Why software testing is important* section).

In addition to this, there is a great possibility of reducing development costs if the testing process starts early on in the cycle. This is because catching defects early can help reduce the costs associated with fixing them later on. Additionally, identifying and addressing issues early in development can help prevent delays and rework, which can also save money.

But money, although the most important, is only one of the reasons why companies should test their software. Software testing is a crucial process in the software development life cycle, as it ensures that the final product is of high quality, meets the customer's requirements, and is mostly free of defects and errors (as we will see in Chapter 4, there is no such thing as a "bug-free" program). Here are some of the other key benefits:

- **Improving software quality**: Testing helps identify defects, errors, and vulnerabilities early in the development process before the software is released. This can prevent issues that would be more costly and difficult to fix later on and ultimately result in a higher quality product.

SOFTWARE TESTING EXPLAINED | 29

- **Enhancing customer satisfaction**: High-quality software that functions as expected can lead to happier customers and better business outcomes.
- **Meeting regulatory and industry standards**: Depending on the industry or domain, software may need to comply with specific regulations or standards. Testing can help ensure that the software meets these requirements and avoid costly penalties or fines.
- **Security**: Software testing helps in identifying security vulnerabilities in the software. This is important as the software can be prone to attacks and hacking if there are security vulnerabilities. By identifying these vulnerabilities early on, software testing helps make the software more secure and less prone to attacks.
- **Quality of the product**: Software testing helps in ensuring that the software meets the quality standards and requirements set by the customer. By testing the software, defects and errors are identified and fixed, which ensures that the final product is of high quality and meets the customer's requirements.
- **Customer satisfaction**: By ensuring that the software meets the quality standards and

requirements set by the customer, software testing helps enhance customer satisfaction. This is important, as satisfied customers are more likely to return and use the software again.

- **Easy while adding new features**: Software testing ensures that the software is easily maintainable and extensible. This means that when new features are added, the software continues to work as expected and does not introduce new defects or errors.

- **Determining software performance**: Software testing helps in determining the performance of the software. This is important as the performance of the software can affect the user experience. By testing the performance of the software, any bottlenecks or performance issues can be identified and fixed.

- **Supporting maintenance and upgrades**: A well-tested software system is easier to maintain and upgrade over time, since issues can be more easily isolated and resolved.

As you can see, there are several reasons why a company should invest in the software testing process. Testing is an essential component of software development that ensures that products are delivered with high quality and meet the desired requirements of customers. Testing helps identify defects or bugs in the software and rectify them before the product is launched into the market. In this way, testing reduces the risk of negative consequences such as loss of revenue, damage to brand reputation, and legal issues that could arise from software failures.

Testing's Contribution to Success

Because of all the reasons that have been previously listed, you might be starting to understand why testing is a crucial aspect of software development. The first and most important reason is that it contributes significantly to the success of a project. Essentially speaking, if you want to have a successful product, testing is a no-brainer in which you should definitely invest.

Another reason for using testing as a tool for success is that it helps ensure that software meets its requirements and is free from defects. By discovering and fixing issues early in the development process, testing helps prevent costly mistakes and delays that can arise if problems are not identified and resolved until later stages of development or even after the software has been deployed. Furthermore, testing ensures that software is secure, reliable, and performs as expected, which can improve user satisfaction, brand reputation, and the overall success of the project.

In addition to this, testing also contributes to the success of a project by enhancing the development process. Through testing, developers can gain a deeper understanding of how the software works and how it can be improved. This knowledge can be used to make informed decisions about new features and enhancements that will improve the software's functionality, usability, and overall quality.

Testing is also essential for determining the performance of software. By testing the software under a range of conditions and scenarios, developers can identify performance bottlenecks and other issues that could affect the software's speed, reliability, and scalability. This knowledge can be used to optimize the software's performance and ensure that it meets the needs of its users.

When you know the user's needs, it also makes it easier to add new features to software. By identifying potential issues, conflicts, and customer demands early on in the development process, testing ensures that new features can be added without causing unexpected problems or conflicts with existing functionality.

Finally, and I cannot express this enough or more emphatically, the most significant benefit of testing is that it helps reduce costs in development. By catching bugs early in the development process, testing saves time and money that would have been spent on debugging and reworking the software later on. It also helps prevent potential damages or losses that can arise from security vulnerabilities or software failures, which could lead to lawsuits, fines, and other legal issues.

Therefore, as you can see, testing's contribution to the success of software development cannot be overstated. By ensuring that software is secure, reliable, and performs as expected, testing improves user satisfaction, brand reputation, and the overall success of a project. Moreover, testing helps reduce costs in development, enhances the development process, makes it easier to add new features, and determines the performance of the software. Thus, it is crucial for people entering or already in the field to understand the importance of testing and its role in achieving success in software development.

TEN REASONS WHY YOU SHOULD BECOME A SOFTWARE TESTER

If you are looking for a new professional challenge and software testing seems like an appealing path to follow,

I want to ensure that this decision will not disappoint. This career can be considered a wise choice, and you don't necessarily need to have a technical background to perform it. As with many careers in the IT industry, there are several courses that offer training, so you can enter the market as soon as you are done. But if you are looking for more incentive, here are 10 reasons why you should become a software tester.

1. **High demand**: As technology continues to evolve, the demand for skilled software testers is on the rise. According to the Bureau of Labor Statistics, employment of software developers is projected to grow 22% from 2019 to 2029, much faster than the average for all occupations (Bureau of Labor Statistics, 2018).

2. **Competitive salary**: As demand for skilled software testers continues to increase, so does the average salary. According to Glassdoor, the average base pay for a software tester in the United States is $76,000 per year (*How Much Does a Software Tester Make?*, 2022).

3. **Opportunity for growth**: A career in software testing can offer a variety of opportunities for growth, from entry-level positions to management roles. There is also potential to specialize in specific areas such as automation

testing, performance testing, and security testing.

4. **Constant learning**: The field of software testing is constantly evolving, which means you will always have new things to learn. You will have to keep up with the latest tools and technologies to stay current. This constant learning will keep you engaged and challenged.

5. **It's challenging**: Software testing requires attention to detail and critical thinking skills. You will have to analyze and solve complex problems, which can be challenging but also very rewarding. The sense of accomplishment when you identify and fix a bug is unparalleled.

6. **Critical role**: Software testing plays a critical role in ensuring the quality, reliability, and functionality of software applications. By becoming a software tester, you are contributing to the success of projects and ultimately helping to build better products for end-users.

7. **Various pathways**: Software testing is a broad field that offers many different career pathways. You can specialize in different areas, such as automation testing, performance testing, security testing, or manual testing. You can also move up to become a Quality

Architect, QA Manager or even a QA Engineer Director.

8. **Get creative**: Software testing involves creating scenarios that test the limits of the software. You get to brainstorm different scenarios and see how the software reacts. This creative aspect of software testing is exciting and rewarding.

9. **Job stability**: Software testing is an essential part of the software development process, meaning that software testers are needed at every stage of a project's life cycle. This job stability can be attractive to individuals who value job security.

10. **No need to know code**: Yes! You read this right! Knowing how to code is not a requirement for all the software testing positions. This means that even if you are not a developer, you can act as a quality assurance or testing professional, opening up the doors to many individuals who want to enter the area but are unsure because they can't or don't know how to code.

With all this information, I bet I have gotten you more excited to learn about this profession, am I right? I am glad to hear this and excited to share with you more details. As you can see, software testing goes beyond the need for coding and technical knowledge, although these will prove to be important, especially if you want to grow in this career. If you combine your dedication, studies, and the knowledge obtained from this book, you will be on a good path to start.

Therefore, without further ado, let's start your journey in the world of software testing. The first stop: learning what the software development lifecycle and the software testing lifecycle are. Read on to find out what these are and why they are so important.

2

SOFTWARE DEVELOPMENT LIFE CYCLE VS. SOFTWARE TESTING LIFE CYCLE

Two of the most important terms in software testing are **software development life cycle (SDLC)** and **software testing life cycle (STLC)**. For potential testers, it is crucial to know what both terms are about, why they are important, and how they differ. To make this first contact with these terms short and objective, we could say that STLC is part of SDLC. STLC is considered a subset of the SDLC, since it is limited to the testing phase, whereas the SDLC is a process used by the software industry to design, develop and test high quality softwares (*Comparison-STLC and SDLC*, n.d.). The SDLC aims to produce high-quality software that meets or exceeds customer expectations, reaches completion within time and cost estimates.

The SDLC consists of various phases like planning, requirements gathering, designing, development, testing, implementation, and maintenance (Martin, 2020). Each phase of the SDLC is critical, and it is essential to follow the steps systematically to ensure the development of quality software. The SDLC starts with the planning phase, where the software requirements are analyzed and a project plan is created. This phase is followed by the requirement gathering phase, where the software requirements are collected from stakeholders. In the design phase, the software architecture is designed. In the development phase, the software is developed, and in the testing phase, the software is tested thoroughly to ensure that it meets the required standards. Finally, the software is implemented, and the maintenance phase ensures that the software continues to function correctly.

The STLC is an integral part of the SDLC. It starts after the software requirements have been gathered and continues until the software has been tested and is ready for deployment. The STLC involves various phases like test planning, test design, test execution, and test closure. In the test planning phase, the testing objectives are defined, and the testing strategy is created. In the test design phase, the test cases are designed based on the software requirements. In the test execution phase, the test cases are executed, and the software is thoroughly tested. Finally, in the test closure phase, the test results are analyzed, and a test report is created.

The importance of following both the SDLC and STLC is crucial to ensuring the development of quality software. Following these processes helps reduce costs and development time by detecting and fixing errors early in the development cycle. It also ensures that the software meets the user requirements and is tested thoroughly before deployment, reducing the risk of software failure.

WHAT IS THE SOFTWARE DEVELOPMENT LIFE CYCLE?

The software development life cycle (SDLC) is a process that is used to design, develop, test, and maintain software applications. It is a framework that provides a structured approach to software development and consists of several phases, each of which has specific goals and deliverables. The typical SDLC consists of six phases:

1. Requirement gathering and analysis
2. Design
3. Implementation or coding
4. Testing

5. Deployment
6. Maintenance

The importance of following a structured SDLC is that it helps to ensure that software applications are developed in a systematic and controlled manner. This helps to reduce errors and defects in the software and ensures that the final product meets the requirements and specifications of the stakeholders. Following the SDLC also helps to improve communication among team members, reduce development time, and ultimately reduce costs.

How the SDLC works

The software development life cycle (SDLC) is a process that outlines the various stages involved in software development, from initial planning to deployment. It serves as a roadmap for the entire software development process and is designed to ensure that the final product meets the specified requirements and is of high quality.

The SDLC usually starts in the planning phase, which involves defining the project scope, goals, and objectives, identifying the stakeholders, and creating a project plan. Next, the SDLC is developed, and it typically consists of the following stages:

1. **Requirements gathering**: In this stage, the project team works with stakeholders to identify the functional and non-functional requirements for the software.
2. **Design**: The design stage involves creating a detailed technical design of the software, including the software architecture, database schema, and user interface design.
3. **Development**: The development stage involves writing code and building the software using the design specifications.
4. **Testing**: In this stage, the software is tested to identify and fix any bugs or issues that might exist.
5. **Deployment**: The software is released and deployed to end-users.
6. **Maintenance**: The software is monitored and maintained to ensure that it continues to function as expected and meets the evolving needs of the end-users.

The SDLC is important because it provides a structured and systematic approach to software development that helps to ensure that the final product meets the requirements and is of high quality. By following the SDLC, development teams can reduce costs, minimize risks, and ensure that the software is delivered on time and within budget—two of the most important aspects clients think of when they are developing a new program.

As you have seen, SDLC has several stages, including planning, analysis, design, implementation, testing, deployment, and maintenance. Each stage involves different activities, deliverables, and best practices. Following SDLC processes helps organizations reduce development costs, increase productivity, improve communication, and minimize project risks. Let's take a deeper look into what each of these stages entails and what the best practices in the market are for them.

Stages and best practices

The SDLC consists of various stages, each with its own set of best practices. Here are the stages and best practices for each stage of the process:

1. **Analysis**: In this stage, the requirements are analyzed in detail, and the functional and non-functional requirements are identified. Best practices include conducting a detailed analysis of requirements, identifying any constraints or limitations, and determining the impact of the project on the existing system.

2. **Design**: In this stage, the design of the system is created and the architectural and detailed designs are developed. Best practices include creating a high-level design, creating a detailed design, and creating a prototype if needed.

3. **Development**: In this stage, the actual coding of the software takes place. Best practices include using a coding standard, conducting code reviews, and using version control.

4. **Testing**: In this stage, the software is tested to ensure that it meets the requirements and works as intended. Best practices include creating test cases, conducting functional and non-functional testing, and conducting user acceptance testing.

5. **Deployment**: In this stage, the software is deployed to the production environment. Best practices include creating a deployment plan, conducting a pilot test, and using automated deployment tools.

6. **Maintenance**: In this stage, the software is maintained and updated to ensure that it continues to meet the changing needs of the users. Best practices include conducting regular maintenance, using a bug-tracking system, and conducting periodic reviews.

Following best practices at each stage of the SDLC is essential to ensure the success of the project and reduce costs in development. By following a well-defined SDLC process, developers can ensure a positive experience with the process and guarantee a quality product for their clients, minimizing the risks and issues they might face due to a lack of investment.

WHAT IS THE SOFTWARE TESTING LIFE CYCLE?

The software testing life cycle (STLC) is a process that software development teams follow to ensure that the software being developed is of high quality, meets the specified requirements, and is reliable and robust (Hamilton, 2023c). It is a set of activities performed by the testing team in a systematic way to detect defects and ensure the quality of the product before it is released.

The STLC includes several phases, including requirement analysis, test planning, test case development, test execution, defect reporting, and test closure (Rajkumar, 2023a). Each phase has its own set of goals and objectives, and each is equally important in ensuring the quality of the software.

By following the STLC, software development teams can reduce the number of defects in the software, improve its quality, and reduce the overall cost of software development. This is because testing is performed throughout the development process, ensuring that defects are caught and fixed early, reducing the cost of fixing defects later in the process.

What Is the Role of the STLC?

The role of the STLC is to provide a systematic and structured approach to the testing of software applications (Synopsys, 2019). The STLC defines a set of activities that are performed during the testing process, from the planning phase to the closure phase. The STLC helps ensure that the software being developed is of high quality, meets business requirements, and is delivered on time and within budget.

The STLC includes several phases, such as requirement analysis, test planning, test case design, test execution, and defect tracking (Rajkumar, 2023a). Each of these phases plays an important role in the overall testing process and helps ensure that the software being developed meets the quality standards set by the organization.

In addition to ensuring the quality of the software, the STLC also helps reduce the overall cost of development. By identifying defects and issues early in the testing process, organizations can avoid costly rework and delays in the development cycle. This, in turn, can lead to faster time-to-market, reduced maintenance costs, and increased customer satisfaction.

The Six STLC Phases in Depth

The STLC consists of six phases that cover the entire testing process, from planning to execution to reporting. As you will see, when these six phases are implemented, they can help reduce costs by identifying and fixing defects early in the development cycle, resulting in higher-quality software (*An Introduction to Software Testing Life Cycle (STLC): Definition and Phases*, n.d.).

- **Requirement analysis**: In this phase, the testing team analyzes the software requirements to identify any potential issues that may arise during the testing process. This phase involves reviewing the requirements documentation and identifying ambiguities, inconsistencies, and conflicts in the requirements. The primary goal of this phase is to understand the software's functional and non-functional requirements and determine how they will be tested.

- **Test planning**: In this phase, the testing team prepares a comprehensive test plan that outlines the testing strategy, test objectives, testing approach, resources required, and timelines for testing. The test plan includes a detailed description of the test scenarios, test cases, test data, and test environment required to carry out the testing. The primary goal of this phase is to develop a detailed test plan that can be executed in a controlled and organized manner.

- **Test case development**: In this phase, the testing team develops test cases based on the requirements and test plan. Test cases are designed to validate the software's functionality, usability, performance, and security. Test cases are typically created using a combination of manual and automated testing methods. The primary goal of this phase is to develop a comprehensive set of test cases that can be used to validate the software's functionality.

- **Test environment setup**: In this phase, the testing team sets up the test environment, which includes hardware, software, and network configurations required for testing. The test environment should be a replica of the production environment to ensure that the test results are accurate and reliable. The primary goal of this phase is to ensure that the test environment is set up correctly to enable efficient and effective testing.

- **Test execution**: In this phase, the testing team executes the test cases developed in the previous phase. The tests are executed based on the test plan and the test cases developed. Test execution involves running the tests, logging the results, and verifying whether the test results meet the expected outcomes. The primary goal of this phase is to identify defects, errors, and issues in the product before it is released to the public.

- **Test closure**: In this phase, the testing team prepares a test closure report that summarizes the testing results, the defects identified, and the test coverage achieved. The report provides valuable insights into the software's quality, which can be used to improve future software development projects. The primary goal of this phase is to evaluate the testing process, identify areas for improvement, and provide recommendations for future testing projects.

What Are the Entry and Exit Criteria in STLC?

Entry and exit criteria are essential components of the STLC. They are used to define the conditions that must be met before entering or exiting a particular stage in the testing process (Rajkumar, 2023a). **Entry criteria** are the set of conditions that must be met before testing can begin, while **exit criteria** are those that must be met before testing can be completed.

Entry criteria are necessary because they help ensure that the testing process is effective and efficient. They help to identify potential issues early on in the testing process, which can help reduce costs and prevent delays. By establishing clear entry criteria, testing teams can avoid wasting time and resources on testing that is not yet feasible.

To illustrate the situation, we can say that the entry criteria for the testing phase might include having a completed software design document and having all necessary resources, such as hardware and software, available for testing. Without these criteria being met, the testing process cannot begin.

Exit criteria are equally important because they help ensure that the testing process is thorough and effective (Pp_pankaj, 2023b). They provide a set of standards that must be met before testing can be considered complete. This helps to ensure that all potential issues have been identified and resolved before the software is released.

For instance, exit criteria for the testing phase might include achieving a certain level of test coverage, resolving all high-priority defects, and obtaining sign-off from key stakeholders. Without these criteria being met, testing cannot be considered complete.

Requirement Phase Testing

The requirement phase is the first phase in software testing and is critical to ensuring that the software meets the needs of the stakeholders (Pp_pankaj, 2023b). In this phase, the software requirements are analyzed and understood to develop the test plan and test cases that will be used to verify the software. During the requirement phase, the testing team works with the development team and stakeholders to identify the requirements and develop the testing strategy. The goal of the testing team is to ensure that the software meets the requirements and that any potential issues are identified early in the development process. This helps reduce the costs and time associated with fixing issues later in the development cycle.

The key activities in the requirement phase include reviewing the requirements, identifying any ambiguities or inconsistencies, developing the test plan and test cases, and ensuring that the testing team has a clear understanding of the requirements.

Some best practices for the requirement phase include:

- Establish clear communication channels between the testing team, development team, and stakeholders to ensure that everyone has a clear understanding of the requirements.
- Use techniques such as interviews, surveys, and workshops to gather information about the requirements and ensure that they are well understood.
- Ensure that the requirements are complete, consistent, and unambiguous.

Test planning in STLC

Test planning is an important phase in the STLC and plays a crucial role in ensuring that the software is of high quality and adequate to be used by the final customer. It involves developing a comprehensive plan to ensure that all aspects of testing are covered, including test objectives, strategy, approach, scope, schedule, environment, and deliverables (Rajkumar, 2023b).

The main objective of test planning is to define how testing will be conducted throughout the development lifecycle, what resources are required, and how to minimize the risk of defects in the software. It also provides a clear understanding of the project requirements and the scope of testing.

Here are the key activities in the test planning phase, according to Hamilton (2023b):

1. **Test plan development**: Test plan development involves defining the test strategy, test objectives, test scope, test approach, test schedule, and test deliverables.
2. **Resource planning**: This involves identifying the required resources for the testing phase, including human resources, hardware, software, and other resources.
3. **Risk analysis**: Risk analysis involves identifying the potential risks that may impact the project, evaluating their likelihood and impact, and developing a plan to mitigate them.
4. **Test environment setup**: The test environment is set up to simulate the production environment and ensure that the software is

tested in an environment similar to the one in which it will be used.

5. **Test case development**: Test cases are developed based on the requirements specification, and they include the test scenarios, test data, expected results, and actual results.

6. **Test execution planning**: This involves planning the test execution and creating a schedule for the testing phase.

The test planning phase is essential in ensuring the success of the testing process. It helps in defining the testing objectives, identifying the resources required, and ensuring that the software is thoroughly tested. Proper planning helps to avoid rework, reduces the cost of testing, and improves the overall quality of the software.

Why Is the STLC Important?

The STLC is an essential part of software development that helps ensure the quality, reliability, and effectiveness of software. It is a systematic process that includes planning, designing, executing, and reporting software testing activities, and it is crucial to reducing costs, improving customer satisfaction, and enhancing business reputation. Due to this, its importance cannot be overstated.

Here are some of the key reasons why the STLC is important:

- **Improves software quality**: By following the STLC, software developers can ensure that the software they produce is of high quality. This is because the process identifies defects and errors in the software at an early stage, allowing developers to address them before they become major problems.
- **Reduces cost**: The STLC helps reduce the cost of software development by catching defects early in the process. This saves time and resources that would otherwise be spent on fixing problems in later stages of development.
- **Improves customer satisfaction**: A product that has been thoroughly tested through the STLC is more likely to meet customer requirements and expectations, resulting in higher levels of client satisfaction.
- **Enhances business reputation**: When software undergoes the STLC, it is less likely to suffer from errors and defects, which can damage the reputation of the business that produced it.

- **Ensures regulatory compliance**: Many industries have regulatory requirements for software development. The STLC helps ensure that these requirements are met and that the software is compliant with regulations.

THE DIFFERENCE BETWEEN SDLC AND STLC

As you might have seen by now, SDLC and STLC are two different concepts related to software development, each with its own significance and importance. While the SDLC is a process for the development of software, the STLC is a process for the testing of software. In other words, SDLC is concerned with how the software is developed, while STLC is concerned with how the software is tested.

To speak in general terms, we could say that the SDLC is a broad concept that includes all the stages involved in the development of software, from gathering requirements to deployment. It consists of six stages: requirements, design, implementation, testing, deployment, and maintenance. The main objective of SDLC is to produce high-quality software that meets the requirements of the customer, is delivered on time and within budget, and is easy to maintain.

The STLC, on the other hand, is a part of the SDLC process and is focused uniquely on testing. It also consists of six stages: requirement analysis, test planning, test design, test execution, test reporting, and closure. The main objective of this process is to ensure that the software is thoroughly tested and meets the quality standards before it is released to the customer.

Therefore, we can conclude that the main difference between SDLC and STLC is their focus. While one is focused on the development of software, the other has as its main objective testing the software. SDLC includes testing as a part of the development process, while STLC is concerned with testing the software as a separate process.

Now that we have already seen the roles of software development and testing, we need to take a step further into what this testing will entail. Essentially speaking, we could say that the main objective is to ensure quality. As you might imagine, these two concepts are closely related, albeit still different. In the next chapter, we will take a look at what it means to have software quality assurance and how this impacts or is impacted by software testing.

3

UNDERSTANDING THE ROLE OF SOFTWARE QUALITY ASSURANCE

Be a yardstick of quality. Some people aren't used to an environment where excellence is expected.

— STEVE JOBS

Quality assurance is an important subject in software development that is closely connected to software testing. It does not matter if you want to get into software testing or software quality assurance; you should know what they are, how these terms are different from one another, and what skills may be beneficial to become great at them.

As you will see in this chapter, software quality assurance (SQA) involves a wide range of activities, such as planning, designing, implementing, executing, and reporting tests (*What Is Software Quality Assurance (SQA): A Guide for Beginners*, 2023). It also includes reviewing the code and documentation to ensure that they meet the required standards and guidelines that the customer or the company has. SQA also plays a crucial role in maintaining the reputation of the software development company—can you imagine the repercussions of delivering a product without quality to your client? They might not return the business to you. On the other hand, a high-quality product that meets the expectations of the users can significantly improve the company's image and attract more customers.

WHAT IS SQA?

As I mentioned earlier, SQA is a systematic process that ensures the quality of software and services through planning, controlling, measuring, evaluating, and reporting the software development. When you apply SQA standards to the development of software, it helps to identify and eliminate any defects or flaws in the product before it is delivered to the customer, as well as reduce development costs, improve the quality of the product that is being developed, and increase client satisfaction (Brewster, n.d.).

The importance of SQA lies in its ability to improve the overall quality of the software and reduce the cost of development. When the developer or the company uses SQA to identify defects and bugs early in the development process, they will prevent costly rework and delays (Gayatri, 2023). It also ensures that the software meets the expectations of the users and fulfills its intended purpose.

SQA Plan

One of the first things that needs to be done when a company wants to implement a quality assurance system is to develop a plan. The SQA plan (SQAP) is a document that outlines the approach, procedures, and resources needed to ensure that software meets the desired level of quality (Simplilearn, 2023). You should think of this plan as a sort of roadmap that outlines the processes and activities that will be used to ensure that the software is tested and verified, together with identifying if it meets the required quality standards.

When you think about the process of creating the SQAP document, you must consider that this initial phase is very important. The main reason for this is that, depending on how you shape it, it will help ensure that the software is reliable, efficient, and meets the established requirements. It will also help identify the risks involved in the development process and provide strategies to reduce them. This plan guarantees several benefits for both the company developing the product and the client who is going to use it.

The SQAP should include the following elements:

1. Objectives and goals of SQA
2. Scope and approach for the SQA process
3. Roles and responsibilities of the SQA team members
4. Methodology to be used for testing and quality assurance
5. Procedures for tracking, reporting, and managing defects
6. Criteria for accepting or rejecting the product
7. Schedule for executing SQA activities
8. Resources needed for SQA activities

Based on the information we have seen, it is possible to say that the SQAP is a vital document. When preparing the SQAP, the company can outline the procedures and activities to be used during the QA process. This will help them ensure that the software meets the required quality standards—both inside and outside the corporation (such as regulatory and market compliance standards). In addition to this, it will help reduce costs and minimize the risks associated with software development, all while ensuring that the product is reliable and efficient.

SQA Activities

When we talk about SQA activities, it is important to understand that these are aimed at identifying and fixing defects and problems in software before delivering the final result. These SQA activities are primarily designed to help reduce costs associated with software development by ensuring that issues are caught and fixed earlier in the development process. When we consider these activities, there are a few common elements that we should consider:

1. **Requirement analysis**: Identification and analysis of customer requirements and their translation into technical specifications
2. **Test planning**: Development of test plans and strategies to ensure that software meets the quality standards and customer requirements
3. **Test execution**: Test execution and performance of test cases to ensure that the software meets the specified quality standards

4. **Defect tracking**: Identification and tracking of defects and deficiencies in software applications throughout the development process

5. **Process improvement**: Identification and implementation of process improvements to improve software development practices and the quality of the software

6. **Audits and reviews**: Performance of audits and reviews of the products and processes to ensure compliance with quality standards

Here, it is important to mention that there are several international certifications that can be applied to ensure that the software is compliant, such as ISO 9000, the Capability Maturity Model Integrated (CMMI) from Carnegie Mellon University, created with the aid of the United States government, and the Testing Maturity Model (TMM) (Brewster, n.d.).

Implementing SQA standards can help organizations improve the quality of their products, reduce costs associated with defects, and increase customer satisfaction. By following established best practices and guidelines, organizations can ensure that their software meets industry standards and is reliable, efficient, and effective.

Elements of Software Quality Assurance

The process of SQA consists of several elements essential for ensuring the quality of software. The importance of these elements lies in their ability to improve the quality of products while reducing costs associated with defects, rework, and maintenance. They include:

1. **Process improvement**: The goal of this element is to continuously improve the software development process by identifying inefficiencies and bottlenecks and implementing best practices to optimize the process.

2. **Quality planning**: Involves the development of a comprehensive plan for ensuring the quality of software. This includes identifying quality objectives, determining the scope of testing, defining testing procedures, and identifying metrics for measuring quality.

3. **Reviews and inspections**: These are critical activities for detecting defects and ensuring that software is built according to specifications. These activities can include code reviews, design reviews, and walkthroughs.

4. **Testing**: Testing is a critical element of SQA and involves the execution of test cases to

ensure that software meets functional and performance requirements.

5. **Training**: This element is essential for ensuring that all members of the software development team understand SQA processes and procedures and are equipped with the skills needed to carry out their roles effectively.

6. **Auditing**: When auditing is carried out, it involves reviewing SQA processes and procedures to identify areas for improvement and ensure that they are being followed consistently.

SQA Techniques

When you consider SQA, there are several techniques that can be used to ensure the quality of the software you are using. These refer to the various methods and tools used to guarantee that the product is of high quality, meets the desired requirements, and performs as expected. Some of the concepts that can be considered for SQA include a variety of tests, such as static, dynamic, and performance testing, which we will see more about further along in this book. In the meantime, I want to approach two themes that were mentioned by Brewster (n.d.): the approaches that SQA has for both defect and attribute management.

Software Quality Defect Management Approach

When you consider defect management, there is a process to identify the "bugs" that you might find in your program. Because of the importance that these bugs can bring to the software and to the user, defect management is seen as an essential aspect of software quality assurance. It is a part of the SDLC and is comprised of the following steps (Nanda, 2021):

1. **Identify or discover**: The first step is to identify and document defects in the software. These can be identified through various means, such as manual testing, automated testing, code review, or user feedback. It is essential that as many of these defects as possible are found while the program has not yet been launched.

2. **Categorize**: Once a defect is identified, it needs to be logged into what is known as a defect tracking system. This system to categorize the issues should include information such as the severity of the defect, the steps to reproduce it, and the person responsible for the resolution. A subcategory of this phase of categorization involves determining the **risk** of the defect and determining if it is low, medium, or high for its maintenance.

3. **Resolution**: Now that the defect has been categorized and prioritized, it needs to be resolved by the appropriate person who has been assigned to it. This individual should have the necessary skills and expertise to fix the defect. Once it has been solved, it is important that the rest of the team is communicated with and that the progress is measured throughout the process.

4. **Verification**: Once a defect is resolved, it needs to be verified to ensure that it has been fixed correctly. This step involves retesting the software to ensure that the defect has been fixed and that it is functioning as expected.

5. **Closure**: Now that the problem has been identified and solved, it can be closed in the defect tracking system. This process indicates that it has been resolved and is no longer an issue.

6. **Reporting**: When you think about reporting the issue, this means that you will issue a document explaining the problem, what caused it, how it was fixed, and how it can be avoided in the future. This is a part of the process improvement and will enable tracking of what is being done and monitoring the status of the software.

By identifying and resolving defects early in the SDLC, software development teams can save time and resources that would otherwise be spent on fixing defects later in the development cycle or after deployment.

Software Quality Attributes Approach

Next, we need to talk about the quality attributes that your software has. This means looking at its several different characteristics and identifying them. According to Brewster (n.d.), depending on the professional that is asked, the number of attributes that need to be measured can vary. For me, here are the eight main non-functional requirements (as these are known, since the system depends on them to be used, but they are not related to what the software in itself does) that should be considered:

1. **Security:** How safe is the program regarding malicious attempts by hackers or information leaks?
2. **Efficiency:** How long does a process take to complete, or does the user need to wait to have an answer to their request?
3. **Performance:** Does the system respond fast to requests and demands?
4. **Usability:** How easy is this system to use?

5. **Functionality:** Does the software meet the requirements? Will it serve its purpose?
6. **Portability:** Can the software run on several platforms?
7. **Reliability:** Is the program one we can trust to bring accurate results?
8. **Maintainability:** How easy is it to administer and maintain the software if needed?

This approach is very important because it enables software development teams to identify the key attributes important for the success of a piece of software. In addition to this, once these requirements are established, they will enable the development team to design, develop, and test the system to meet these requirements, helping reduce the risk of project failure due to poor quality.

Why Is Software Quality Assurance Important?

As you have read from many of the reasons that I just told you about, SQA is one of the most important processes that a company must invest in to ensure that their product is the best possible for the client. It should be made a priority among those who work in the software development industry—and for those who wish to enter it as well. Applying the SQA framework to your software means that it is more reliable, effective, and efficient, as well as reducing costs in rework and maintenance.

Just to recap a little, let's make a short list of reasons for the importance of SQA:

- prevents software problems in final delivery
- ensures software efficiency and effectiveness
- establishes quality of the final product
- helps save costs
- increases reliability for the developing company
- makes software safer

In summary, for those who want to enter the software development field or who are already working in it, understanding the importance of SQA can help set you apart from others who may not prioritize quality in their work. Employers look for candidates who understand the importance of SQA and have experience implementing its processes, see their careers advance, and increase their value to employers.

But knowing this will likely bring you to the next question: *What is the difference between software testing and quality assurance?* This is a completely valid question, and it makes sense that you would ask it. Keep on reading because this is the next thing I will explain.

THE DIFFERENCE BETWEEN SOFTWARE TESTING AND QUALITY ASSURANCE

If you are thinking that the concepts of SQA and software testing are similar, let me tell you that this is not uncommon. Many people confuse both topics, but I have a definition I once read in Simonova (2022) that will help make it clear: "Software testing assists with finding and fixing already existing errors, while QA helps prevent them. Both of these processes play an important role in achieving optimum quality; they complement each other." Makes it easier to understand, correct?

Essentially speaking, if you confuse them, you are not far off from the mark. Software testing and SQA are both important aspects of product development, although they serve different purposes. I could define software testing as the process of identifying defects or bugs in software by running tests on it. These tests can be manual or automated and can be carried out throughout several parts of the development process. When you carry out software testing, your main objective will be to identify and fix defects before the software is released to users (Wilk, 2020).

On the other hand, I would define SQA as the process of ensuring that software products meet their specified requirements and are as free as possible from defects. When you consider this process, you should think that it involves the development of processes, procedures, and standards so that the software you will present to the final client is of high quality. From this viewpoint, we could say that SQA can include testing, but it also includes other activities such as requirements gathering, design reviews, code reviews, and process audits. The goal of SQA is to ensure that software is reliable, effective, and efficient, and meets the needs of its users (Sharma, 2022).

To conclude, I could say that software testing and SQA are both important and complementary aspects of software development. Once you implement both of these in your development process, it can help reduce costs and improve software quality. By now, you must be thinking, *What do I need to do to become a SQA professional?* Well, that is a very good question. Read on to find out what skills and characteristics favor those who want to start working in this market.

SKILLS THAT ARE BENEFICIAL TO HAVE WHEN WORKING IN SOFTWARE QUALITY ASSURANCE

When you consider becoming an SQA professional, there is a certain skill set that is interesting to have in order to achieve success. Because these individuals will be responsible for several different processes, such as defining and establishing quality standards, identifying and reporting defects, and creating and applying test strategies, there are characteristics that help them have a more successful approach to the subject.

In my opinion and based on information from several market experts, here are the essential skills one must have to become a successful SQA professional.

1. **Communication:** When you are an SQA professional, it is likely that you will need to interact with the different parties involved in the software development process, such as developers, product owners, and testers. This means that having effective communication skills that can change according to your audience will help ensure that everyone involved in the project is on the same page and can lead to improved collaboration, reduced misunderstandings, and better software quality.

2. **Team player:** The SQA professional does not work alone. Therefore, you must consider the development team, management, and the project manager, for example. Being a team player is an important characteristic to have that will be enhanced by your communication skills. When you are a team player, you will work with the group toward a satisfactory presentation of the final product and ensure client satisfaction. Getting along with everyone, or at least respecting all parties and working together, will be essential for a smooth SQA process.

3. **Organization:** Since the process is long and will possibly include many details, it is essential that the SQA professional is organized. You need to be able to understand the process, identify and log the problems you find, and work according to the plan that was established in the SQAP. Things will need to be followed in a certain order so that the process is effective and, therefore, being organized and able to obtain the information quickly will help in the process.

4. **Discipline:** Related to the previous topic, being a disciplined professional will help you meet the established deadlines with high-quality

solutions. This means being able to follow processes, standards, and procedures and developing ways of making the workflow more efficient.

5. **Attention to detail:** Being able to pay attention to small details is essential if you want to become a professional in SQA. These professionals must be precise to ensure that software products meet their specified requirements and are free from defects. This skill helps them identify and fix issues early in the development process, leading to improved software quality and reduced costs.

6. **Curiosity:** Because curious people are more likely to ask questions, explore alternatives, and experiment with new ideas, they have one of the main traits needed to become an SQA professional. Due to the questions they ask, they can find alternatives to problems and identify new issues that were not foreseen by other members of the team. This will lead to improved software quality because they have anticipated any quality-related problems that the program might have.

7. **Critical and analytical thinking :** Being able to look at a problem, analyze its reasons, and make informed decisions is one of the key

characteristics companies look for when they are searching for SQA professionals. This means that you will be able to digest information and propose effective solutions to problems that you might identify.

8. **Fast learner:** Technology moves fast, and new and innovative ideas are always appearing in the market. Because of this speed and the demand clients have to have their software ready as fast as possible, being a quick learner who will speed up the process will be a quality that will be highly appreciated by companies. This means that you quickly understand what needs to be done and carry out the process efficiently by understanding the requirements and the customer's needs.

9. **Flexibility and creativity:** Just as it is important to be a fast learner because technology is constantly changing, it is also essential to be flexible and be able to analyze the different solutions that there can be to a problem. This means accepting input from other individuals involved in the process and adjusting to new issues that might arise throughout the SQA process. Here, being a creative person will be highly appreciated

because you will be able to think about out-of-the-box solutions.

10. **Accuracy:** If you are documenting a bug issue in the software, you must be accurate. Because changing one item of the product might affect how the whole process is developed, it is essential that you have the ability to get directly to the point and be as accurate as possible regarding what the problem is and how to solve it. When you apply accuracy to your SQA process, this will save time in finding solutions and resolving the issues that might be encountered.

Extra skill: Coding. While knowing how to code is not an essential skill for those who wish to enter the SQA market, it is certainly one that will help. Although coding is not needed to start, especially if you begin as a manual tester, with time and as you increase your knowledge, coding will become more important and will help you advance in your career. In other words, it is not a must, but it is becoming increasingly important for testers to understand and have hands-on experience with coding.

If you understand programming, this will make it easier to understand the process and the logic of what the developer did for the program, and it might even make it easier to fix certain problems because you will know how to get to their root cause. In addition to this, when you know how to code , you can increase the groups you speak to by being both technical with the development team and speaking in a more layperson's vocabulary to the customer, for example.

4

SOFTWARE TESTING MYTHS AND
TRUTHS

> The computer was born to solve problems that
> did not exist before.
>
> — BILL GATES

There are a lot of myths out there about the software testing industry. Have you ever heard any that you can remember? In this chapter, we will uncover the realities behind those myths and show you that misconceptions about the process can lead to ineffective testing and higher development costs.

MYTH 1: SOFTWARE QUALITY IS THE EXCLUSIVE RESPONSIBILITY OF THE TESTER

The first thing I would like to address is one of the most common software testing myths: the belief that software testers are the only ones responsible for ensuring software quality. As you have seen in the previous chapter, in which we talked about SQA, this is certainly not true. While software testers play an important role in identifying defects and ensuring that the final product meets quality standards, they are just one part of a larger quality assurance process.

Here, you must look at the bigger picture and consider that when you are talking about developing software, this will require a team that includes developers, project managers, and stakeholders, to name a few examples. All of these people mentioned, as well as other members that the team might have, must work as a team to ensure that quality is built into the software development process from the beginning. Therefore, we could say that the software tester is **also** responsible for quality, but they are **not the only ones**.

When the company, the team, or even the client fails to understand this myth, it can lead to ineffective testing or even the incorrect allocation of resources during the project. For example, if testers are solely responsible for quality, they may focus solely on testing without considering the overall development process, leading to defects being missed or not properly addressed. This would lead to a product with lower quality and, very likely, a dissatisfied client—and we don't want that at all! By incorporating quality practices into the entire development process, from requirements gathering to release, defects can be caught earlier and with greater accuracy, ultimately leading to a better product.

MYTH 2: TESTING ENSURES 100% BUG-FREE SOFTWARE

The next myth I want to talk about is one that we have seen briefly in the first chapter: that testing will make the final product completely "bug free." I am sorry to be the bearer of bad news, but there is no such thing as 100% bug-free software in every single project you work on. *Why?* You might ask. Well, consider that software development is a complex process that involves several factors that include: changing user requirements, unexpected interactions between different components, and many other unforeseen conditions.

Does this mean that my software will always have bugs? No, definitely not. It will have fewer bugs, but it is impossible to ensure that it will be completely free from them until it goes into production and starts being used.

Users might have different behaviors and means to use it, leading to potential problems that were not anticipated. While software testers strive to find and eliminate as many bugs as possible, it's important to recognize that some bugs will inevitably slip through the cracks. In fact, some bugs may not be discovered until the software is in use by actual users.

If the client is unclear about this, it is important to establish this concept from the beginning. Failing to do so and a bug being subsequently identified can lead the company to have several issues with customers regarding reliability and customer satisfaction. It is also important that, although bug-free is not a guarantee, the whole team involved in the SDLC adopt a mindset of continuous improvement and work to minimize the impact of defects through effective testing and feedback mechanisms. By acknowledging the reality of software development, teams can better manage their resources and build more resilient and adaptable software. Speaking about bugs, this brings me to the next myth: Finding bugs is all a tester does.

MYTH 3: TESTING IS ONLY ABOUT FINDING ERRORS AND BUGS

Let me start by saying: No, this is completely not true. Testing is much more than finding errors and bugs, and

SOFTWARE TESTING EXPLAINED | 85

I will tell you why. When software is developed, someone needs to ensure that it is working according to the client's requirements and that it is functioning as expected. While this may lead to finding some bugs along the way, it does not mean that the **only** intention that the tester will have is to search for them.

The first thing you should **always** remember is that testing is not just about finding defects but is also about ensuring that software meets the functional and non-functional requirements of its users and, of course, that it is of **high quality**. Testers must have a comprehensive understanding of the users' needs and be able to test the software against these.

In addition to this, testers need to ensure that software is user-friendly, accessible, and performs well under different conditions. At the same time, other requirements such as security, performance, and scalability, among others, must be taken into consideration during the testing phase. Testing involves a range of knowledge and expertise, including technical, analytical, and communication skills. Because of these reasons, and to ensure that there are no extra costs, the tester should be involved in the process from the beginning, not only at the end of the development, taking us to our next myth: Testers should only be reached out to once the project is ready.

MYTH 4: TESTERS ARE ONLY INVOLVED AFTER THE SOFTWARE IS READY

While this is something that many companies think is true and proceed this way, if your idea is to save costs and optimize the development process, you should consider incorporating testers at the beginning of the project—yes, from the gathering requirements phase. The main reason for this is that effective software testing requires collaboration between the team during the entire software development lifecycle. Professional testers can provide valuable input into potential issues early on, allowing for proactive measures to be taken to prevent them.

When the company involves testers early in the development process, any potential costs incurred by fixing defects can be reduced, as bugs are more expensive to fix the later they are discovered. It is also an assurance for the client that their product is being tested throughout the full process to ensure that all requirements are met. Testers can also help ensure that software requirements are met, reducing the risk of costly rework or redesign due to bad design or usability issues.

I bet that you didn't know this, right? If you didn't, don't worry. Most people don't. Some individuals from outside this market think that testing is finding issues with the software by clicking relentlessly in random places of the software and waiting to see how it reacts. And this, I must say, brings us to our next myth.

MYTH 5: TESTING IS JUST CLICKING IN RANDOM PLACES

I can assure you that this is not testing. In fact, I do not know of a tester who proceeds this way, since there is a plan and a program to carry out testing. Remember how I said that there needs to be proper documentation to register bugs? Well, when you are testing, you also need to document the process that you went through so that those in charge of fixing the issues can identify what needs to be done.

The truth is that testing is a systematic and structured process that requires a deep understanding of the application being tested as well as knowledge of several testing techniques and methodologies. Testers create what are known as "test cases" based on requirements and different user workflows. This will lead them to execute tests and report any defects or usability issues they find. This whole process is done with the other members of the team to ensure that the product meets user requirements.

Based on this information, you might be thinking that testing can be quite boring. I assure you that it is not. And let me tell you one more thing: The best testers are those who have the most creativity! I know, right? Although it might seem improbable, this is true. Testing is far from being a monotonous activity that does not require imagination. If you consider that you need to "play the role" of the user, this will make you assume different approaches, which makes creativity, as you will now see, one of the essential traits of a tester.

MYTH 6: TESTING REQUIRES NO CREATIVITY

The myth of the testing professional glued to a computer systematically clicking buttons is both untrue and biased. This myth can be harmful as it undermines the value of testing and can discourage people from pursuing careers in the area. In this case, the first thing that needs to be addressed is that testing involves more than just running the same set of tests repeatedly. It requires creativity to design test cases that cover all possible scenarios, including edge cases and user inputs. Imagine that a software program is used by millions of users—you cannot expect that they will all behave the same, and it is the task of the tester to ensure that the most possible scenarios are tested.

For this, testers need to think outside the box and anticipate potential issues that may appear during the development process. This requires the ability to come up with unique solutions to test each of its parts effectively. Professionals in this area need to understand the project's goals and objectives and work closely with the development team to ensure that they understand them. It is an exciting and challenging field that requires a combination of technical expertise, communication skills, and creativity.

MYTH 7: SOFTWARE TESTING IS EXPENSIVE

Finally, we arrive at the final myth: that testing is expensive. Well, it is not necessarily a myth, because this process will have a cost to the company, but I want you to think about the following: What will be the impact on the client if the software is **not** tested? When you think about it this way, you might see that the costs of testing may not be as relevant as the potential impact that a mistake can have on the company and its reputation.

In fact, when you carry out testing, you will not only help preserve the company's image and prevent problems, but you will also reduce costs during the development phase by catching defects early on. It should be considered an investment. As I mentioned earlier, finding and fixing bugs in later stages of development can be much more expensive than catching them during testing. Therefore, when you test your new software thoroughly, it is possible to identify issues before they impact the end users, consequently saving time.

5

COMMON TYPES OF SOFTWARE TESTING

> *The first 90% of the code accounts for the first 90% of the development time. The remaining 10% of the code accounts for the other 90% of the development time.*

— TOM CARGILL

As you might know by now, software testing is an essential part of the software development process before it is released to the public. If you are starting to get interested in this profession or are already working in it, it is essential to understand the common types of software testing. The most common types of software testing are functional, performance, security, usability, and compatibility testing, although there are several others that we will see and talk about in the following chapters (*Types of Software Testing*, n.d.).

However, to give you a quick idea of what each of these is, we could say that:

- **Functional testing** ensures that software functions according to the user's requirements and meets the specified functionality criteria.
- **Performance testing** evaluates the software's response time, speed, stability, scalability, and reliability under different conditions.
- **Security testing** (as the name might suggest) checks the software's security features, such as authentication, authorization, and data confidentiality.
- **Usability testing** ensures that the software is easy to use, intuitive, and accessible to users.
- **Compatibility testing** ascertains that the software is compatible with different operating systems, devices, and browsers.

In this chapter of the book, we are going to see some of these common testing types, the difference between manual and automated testing, what mobile testing is and why it is important, and new-to-the-market gaming and AI testing. But if you still want more information about testing, don't worry! We will address several other testing types, dividing them into functional and non-functional sections in Chapters 6 and 7, respectively. If you are ready to really start getting into the subject and discover all the different options it can offer, prepare yourself—you are about to find out how and why right now!

MANUAL TESTING

As the name suggests, manual testing is the process of verifying and validating software applications or systems manually without the use of automation tools (Meyer, 2022). This type of testing is performed by a human tester who executes test cases and scenarios to identify any defects or issues in the software. The tester usually behaves as the final user would and tries to simulate the process as it would be done by those using the software. By principle, I think you can already imagine why this type of testing is important: *Do you think a machine would be able to perform exactly the same tasks as a human when testing?*

They might. However, when you carry out manual testing, it allows testers to identify defects and issues that may not be detected through automated testing. Yes, machines are not exactly able to foresee exactly how a user would use the software. In addition to this, it is also crucial for ensuring that the software meets the functional and non-functional requirements of its users. Think of it this way: If a human does not test it, how can we be sure that the software is usable for a person?

To perform manual testing, professionals in this field need to have a deep understanding of the software, its features, and its users—what should they expect? They also need to have a solid understanding of testing methodologies, cases, and scenarios. Because of this, this type of testing plays a critical role in software development, despite the advancements in automation testing tools. A computer might not be able to see features such as the usability, accessibility, and compatibility of the software it is testing. It also allows testers to explore the software in different ways, which can help identify potential issues that may not be caught through automated testing. Essentially speaking, completely automating a test is impossible (*Manual Testing*, n.d.).

Next, if you think about the non-functional requirements of the system, such as performance and the time it takes to react to a command, this needs to be evaluated by a human. An automated test probably won't mind if the request takes time, but this will be crucial for a human user. Furthermore, these tests are often too complex to be automated, and manual testing is necessary to ensure that the software performs as expected in different environments. *But how is this testing carried out?*

As I mentioned earlier, forget about the professional that is in front of the computer clicking away. According to *Manual Testing* (n.d.), to carry out a manual testing procedure, a few steps, which we will now see, must be observed and taken into consideration.

1. **Understanding the requirements:** A tester needs to understand the requirements of the software they are testing. This includes knowing the expected behavior of the software as well as any user requirements.
2. **Developing test cases:** These should be developed based on the requirements of the software. Test cases should cover all possible scenarios and be designed to identify any defects in the software.
3. **Executing test cases:** Once the test cases have been developed, they must be executed manually by the tester. This involves following the steps outlined in the test case and verifying the expected results.
4. **Recording defects:** If a defect is found during testing, it should be recorded in a defect

tracking tool. This will allow the development team to address the defect and fix it in a timely manner. It is at this step that the development team is informed of the defects so they can fix them.

5. **Retesting:** After a defect has been fixed by the development team, the test case should be executed again to ensure that the defect has been resolved.

Now that you understand what manual testing is, let's take a look at what can be considered the opposite of this process: automated testing.

AUTOMATION TESTING

Automation testing is the process of using software tools, programs, and scripts to execute test cases automatically, as opposed to manually executing them (Meyer, 2022). This type of testing uses tools and scripts to execute test cases for software and applications automatically, without the need for human intervention. When you use this approach, it will involve creating test scripts that can simulate user actions with the application or software that is being tested. One of the advantages is that these scripts can test the software's functionality and identify potential issues or defects repeatedly and continuously.

One of the many advantages of automation testing is that it can be used to test both functional and non-functional aspects of the software, including performance, security, and scalability. Another advantage is that when the testing process is automated, it becomes relatively faster than doing it manually. Finally, I could also mention that automated tests might be more accurate because they are carried out by a machine that will only make mistakes if there is an error in the code. This code, by the way, can also be used for other features and applications, making it reusable for other test cases.

Another advantage is its efficiency, enabling the tests to be performed faster when compared to manual testing. Think about it this way, while a human tester takes time to manually perform the tests, a machine can run continuously until it is told to stop, saving time in labor. This means saving time and costs for the company as well as releasing the software faster to the customer. In addition to this, these tests will be more accurate because they are carried out by a machine, and in many cases, they will catch bugs and defects that otherwise might be missed by the human tester.

Because of their ability to carry out repetitive tests that could be time-consuming and tiresome, automated tests should be applied to a few situations where having the software manually tested would become a laborious task. One example of this would be integration tests, where the script would check how the different parts of the program integrate in functionality with each other. You could also use an automated test to measure how much time each request takes and how much demand it can support. In both of these instances, using a computer to simulate several requests at once or a large number of users accessing the program at the same time makes more sense than using a human tester.

Finally, when you think about the advantages of automated testing, you need to consider that testing using automation will make it easier to catch mistakes and defects early. When they are incorporated into unit testing, for example, as you will see in the next chapter of this book, they enable the developers and testers to test specific parts of the code that can present problems. When this is carried out, it makes it easier for the teams involved to address the issues before they go into operation and fix any potential bugs found, reducing the possibility of a project failure or delay.

Therefore, when you consider testing, you must always think about the possibility of carrying out automated tests where possible, especially to make the feedback more timely. It can also be a "pre-test" of sorts that would evaluate the whole process of the software, leaving the manual testing for more specific areas. This tends to increase productivity and lead the tester to conduct only targeted tests for determined features. Finally, if you consider that you will need one person to monitor the computer's work rather than having a team carry out the tests, this could end up saving some money for the company and the project in general.

MOBILE TESTING

Mobile testing is the process of testing mobile applications on various devices and operating systems to ensure their functionality, usability, and performance (Shain, 2021). Think about how many mobile phones there are in the world today. The question would usually be, "Who **doesn't** have one," right? Considering this and the increasing use of mobile devices for daily activities, the demand for mobile applications has skyrocketed, making mobile testing a critical aspect of software development.

The importance of mobile testing lies in ensuring that the application is bug-free, compatible with various devices and operational systems, user-friendly, and meets the business requirements. Mobile testing can help reduce the cost of development and maintenance as well as help maintain the reputation of the company, especially when many of these software apps have ratings and evaluations made by users in their application stores. Think about how damaging it could be if your company's application had bad reviews from the users: Who do you think will feel the appeal to download and use it?

Apart from the different operating systems that can be used and how the application reacts to them, there are also a few other elements that must be considered. These apps must perform well under varied conditions, such as different screen sizes and resolutions. They should also be able to be used in compatibility with other services (if needed), making it essential to test how they will operate with other applications. Users tend to want things to be as automatic as possible and use the least number of clicks to get what they want, and testing the mobile application will be essential to ensuring this experience.

Next, there are two final items that I want you to consider when you think about mobile testing. The first relates to the differences in network connectivity that need to be considered, since this can vary depending on the location and the service provider. This makes it crucial to test your mobile application under different network conditions, such as 2G, 3G, 4G, and Wi-Fi, to ensure that it performs well under different network conditions.

Secondly, these programs and applications must be safe. Think about the last time you used a mobile app. How much personal information did it request from you? Do you remember linking it to your email account? Did you give it permission to access your contacts and your photos, for example? Therefore, you must remember that mobile devices store sensitive and personal information, and security is critical. Therefore, it's essential to conduct security testing to identify vulnerabilities and guarantee that your application is safe.

If you are interested in getting into the field of mobile testing or are already in the field, remember that it will be essential to stay up to date with the latest tools and techniques to ensure effective and efficient testing.

PERFORMANCE TESTING

The next type of testing I am going to talk about is **performance testing**. Performance testing is a crucial aspect of software testing that focuses on testing the speed, stability, and scalability of a software application under varying load conditions. This means that in this test, you will see how the software reacts if there are a significant number of users making requests at the same time. This is considered an essential step in the software development lifecycle that helps ensure the application meets the requirements of end-users.

Because it is directly related to the user, performance testing is crucial, especially in ensuring that software applications, systems, and websites can perform efficiently and effectively under normal and high load (demand) conditions. Performance testing helps identify and address performance-related issues before the software is deployed to the final audience. Two of its most important factors are maintaining customer satisfaction and increasing the credibility of the application.

If performance testing is something that you would consider getting into, know that it is essential to learn the fundamentals of performance testing, such as identifying the different types of testing, understanding its life cycle, and selecting the appropriate tools. For those who are already in the area, it is essential to keep up with the latest industry trends and technologies to ensure that they deliver high-quality performance testing services.

Some of the factors that a person should know to carry out effective performance testing include:

1. **Response time:** The time taken by an application to respond to user requests
2. **Throughput:** The number of requests that an application can handle per unit of time
3. **CPU usage:** The amount of CPU resources used by an application during its operation
4. **Memory utilization:** The amount of memory used by an application during its operation
5. **Error rate:** The percentage of errors encountered during the testing
6. **Network latency:** The time taken by data to travel from the server to the client
7. **Concurrent users:** The number of users that can access the application simultaneously
8. **Transactions per second:** The number of transactions that an application can process per second
9. **Page load time:** The time taken by a web page to load completely
10. **Server response time:** The time taken by a server to respond to requests

Just like other types of testing, performance testing has a process that needs to be carried out for it to be done.

While these might vary with each company and the strategy that is implemented by the development team, this process is usually comprised of the following eight steps:

1. **Identify the testing environment:** The first thing you will need to do is identify the testing environment, including the system configuration, network infrastructure, and software and hardware configurations.

2. **Determine the testing objectives:** Here, you will determine the objectives of the performance testing—the **what**. These objectives include identifying the response time, throughput, resource utilization, and stability of the system.

3. **Plan and design the performance tests:** Design the test cases to meet the testing objectives. This includes defining the performance metrics, test data, scenarios, and the testing tools.

4. **Configure the test environment:** In this phase of the process, the tester must configure the test environment, including the hardware and software, network configuration, and test tools.

5. **Implement the test design:** Time for action! It is in this phase that the tester will implement the test cases and run the tests.

6. **Analyze the results:** Here, the complete team will evaluate the performance test results to determine the system's performance, including the response time, throughput, resource utilization, and stability.

7. **Optimize the system:** Based on the analysis of the test results, the development team should optimize the system to improve its performance.

8. **Retest and validate:** Retest the system to validate the optimization and ensure that the system meets the performance requirements.

As you can see, most of the steps are going to be similar to other testing schemes, although these will require a little more technical knowledge, such as knowing how to set up the network and understanding its configurations. However, this will not be the only type of testing that will require this knowledge. In the next type of testing we will see, **security testing**, the tester will also need to have a deep understanding of the system and potential threats, since this is considered one of the most important tasks that will need to be carried out.

SECURITY TESTING

Security testing is an essential aspect of software testing that aims to identify vulnerabilities, threats, and risks to the security of an application or system (*Security Testing*, n.d.). This type of testing is essential for ensuring the protection of sensitive data and preventing potential security breaches. In today's ever-growing digital world, testing security in applications and software has become more critical than ever, and it should be a must in all parts of any software development lifecycle.

The main objective of security testing is to identify vulnerabilities and weaknesses in a software system, network, or application that can be used as a means of access by malicious attackers—hackers. When the software or application is secure, this means that sensitive and personal data will be protected. The process involves a series of tests, including penetration testing, vulnerability assessment, and risk assessment, to identify potential security threats and their likelihood of occurrence.

Security testing is essential for web applications because it helps identify vulnerabilities and weaknesses that could be exploited by attackers. By conducting security testing, you can ensure that your web application is secure and meets regulatory requirements. Think about it this way: Web applications have become an essential part of our daily lives, from online banking and shopping to social media and work collaboration tools. It is essential to keep all these applications and information safe.

Some of the key areas of this type of testing include:

1. **Authentication and authorization:** This involves testing the ability of the system to properly identify and authenticate users, as well as ensuring that access to data and functionality is properly controlled and authorized.
2. **Confidentiality:** This area involves testing to ensure that sensitive information is properly protected from unauthorized access or disclosure, both in transit and at rest.
3. **Integrity:** This means testing to ensure that data and systems are not tampered with or modified inappropriately, either intentionally or unintentionally.
4. **Availability:** Testing availability is important to ensure that systems are available and accessible when they are needed and that they can withstand various types of attacks and other disruptions.

5. **Compliance:** Lastly, testing compliance is important to ensure that systems are in compliance with relevant laws, regulations, and industry standards.

To evaluate each of these steps, a series of rigorous processes need to be carried out. This approach needs to be somewhat systematic so that all potential vulnerabilities are identified, addressed, and corrected. Here are some steps to perform security testing (Zuci Systems, 2022):

1. **Identify** potential security risks and vulnerabilities in the application.
2. **Prioritize** and **categorize** the identified risks based on their severity and potential impact.
3. **Develop** test scenarios and test cases that cover the identified vulnerabilities.
4. **Conduct penetration testing** to simulate real-world attacks and identify any weaknesses.
5. **Perform vulnerability scanning** and code analysis to identify potential vulnerabilities in the code.
6. **Test authentication and authorization** mechanisms to ensure that only authorized users have access to the application.

7. **Test data security measures** such as encryption, masking, and hashing to ensure that sensitive data is protected.
8. **Conduct security testing** at different levels, such as network, application, database, and system levels.

GAME TESTING

When you think about the internet and computers, something that might come to mind are the games played on the computer or on the mobile phone. Whether this is because you like to play or you have siblings or children that do, games have become an important part of the tech world and, due to this, a specific type of testing was developed for this market. For you to understand the importance of games, Bultman (2022) mentions a study that says the number of gamers increased by almost 20 million players when comparing the numbers from 2019 and 2020. In addition to this, the study says that the number of players should reach almost 215 million by 2025.

Known as **game testing**, this process is an essential part of game development, and it involves testing a game to ensure it meets specific quality standards before it's released to the public. If you are a player, you know that nothing is worse than playing a game and then encountering a bug or having it present an error right in the middle of its most important part!

When a tester proceeds with testing a game, they are assessing some aspects of the game such as functionality, performance, stability, usability, and compatibility. This will ensure it delivers a seamless and enjoyable gaming experience. Game testing is crucial to ensure that the game is as free as possible of bugs and glitches and that it works as intended on various platforms and devices (remember, there is no such thing as bug-free software!). If you've ever played a game online and the screen just "froze," you know how frustrating this is. Game testing is used to prevent these "freezing bugs" from happening.

In many ways, game development is different from developing common software. It starts in its development cycle, which is considerably different than that of software. In this case, it can be considered a mixture of movie development and software development since its phases will comprise pre-production, production, testing, and release. Because of this, the testing of a game will be different than general software, being comprised of the following:

1. **User experience:** When you consider the user experience, this is one of the most crucial aspects of game testing since the overall satisfaction of the player will determine the success of the game. Unlike with other software, where the user experience is important but not necessarily the top priority, game testing focuses heavily on the user experience, such as game mechanics, graphics, sound, and story.

2. **Complex scenarios:** Game testing involves testing complex scenarios, such as different paths in the game, different levels of difficulty, and various combinations of gameplay. Unlike other types of software, which have limited scenarios, games have a vast range of possibilities, making game testing more challenging.

3. **Compatibility testing:** When you consider the different games that exist, you must know that they are developed for multiple platforms, including desktop, mobile, and consoles. Because of this, game testers need to ensure that the game functions seamlessly across all platforms, including compatibility with various hardware, software, and operating systems.

4. **Non-linear flow:** When the non-linear flow is analyzed, this means that the user can make different choices that impact the outcome of the game. Game testers need to ensure that the game functions correctly, regardless of the choices made by the user.

5. **Dynamic environment:** Games have a dynamic environment, which means the game world changes based on the user's actions. For example, in a game like Minecraft, the game world changes based on what the player builds. Game testers need to ensure that the game world changes correctly without any glitches.

Once these tests are performed, the tester will be able to determine the status of some of the main metrics that need to be considered. These are known as performance indicators, which game testers use to evaluate and measure the success of a game. Knowing these metrics and understanding how to analyze them will provide valuable insights into how the game is being used and can help identify areas for improvement. Some of these include:

1. **Player retention:** This metric measures how many players return to the game after their initial session. It helps identify how engaging

the game is and how likely players are to come back and play it again. A low retention rate can indicate that the game needs improvement.

2. **Time spent playing:** This indicator will help determine how engaging the game is and how long players are willing to play it. It is important to identify the optimal time players are willing to spend in the game.

3. **Conversion rate:** When this metric is applied, it will help the tester to identify players who complete a specific action in the game, such as making a purchase or reaching a certain level. It helps to identify how effective the game is in getting players to take action.

4. **Bug reports:** This metric measures the number of bugs found in the game. It is important to identify and fix bugs as soon as possible to improve the overall user experience.

5. **Load time:** Considered one of the most important metrics in game testing, load time measures how long it takes for the game to load. A long load time determination is important because it can lead to player frustration and discourage them from playing the game.

As you can see, testing games is an important part of the process and is a market that is currently in high demand because of the constant increase in the number of gamers. Professionals that have these skills will be able to identify compatibility, performance, security, user interface, and game balance issues that will help guarantee that the player has a good experience with the game and keeps coming back to it. Finally, consider game testing as an important investment to protect the reputation of the game. The gamer community is close, and having a bad experience with a game will likely discourage other users from engaging with it.

AI TESTING

With advances in technology, you must have been wondering by now whether artificial intelligence (AI) is applied in software testing. Well, let me tell you that it certainly is! And I should say that this form of testing has become a critical area in software testing. It deals with verifying and validating the performance of AI-based systems that are transforming industries and revolutionizing the way we interact with technology. Due to these reasons, the importance of AI testing cannot be overstated.

Consider that although AI can be used for testing and improving automation processes because of its limitations, using it can also be an automatic process (Kirilenko, 2022). Machine learning tools and other bot tools will be helpful, but have you ever thought about who tests the AI programs that we are using?

When professionals carry out this testing process, it helps identify issues, errors, and vulnerabilities in AI models, ensuring that they are safe, accurate, and effective. For those interested in entering this field or for those already working in it, staying up-to-date with the latest AI testing techniques and technologies can help reduce costs and improve the overall quality of AI-based software products.

When you are using AI to test your software, you can consider using it to generate test cases and execute the tests themselves. It can also be used to predict possible defects that the software or program might present by optimizing the testing environment. Having AI test your software will save you time and money—it is an escalation of the automation process. Finally, consider that when you employ AI to carry out the tests, you can also program it to deliver the analysis of the results by generating reports, identifying patterns and trends in software quality, and providing insights to help developers improve the application.

On the other hand, if you are considering becoming a professional that tests AI, you must think about searching for organizations that invest in AI-based testing tools and technologies. These companies usually hire skilled AI testing professionals and provide training for their existing teams. In addition to this, these businesses collaborate with AI testing vendors and consultants who have experience in the field.

Organizations that are successful in promoting AI testing focus on integrating these types of tests, leveraging AI to provide continuous feedback throughout the software development lifecycle. It is important to understand that AI testing is here to stay and will only continue to grow in importance in the years to come.

The following are some steps to take in order to fully embrace the future of AI testing:

1. **Learn:** The first step is to learn as much as possible about AI and its application in testing. This includes understanding the different types of AI, their strengths and limitations, and the various tools and platforms available for AI testing.

2. **Explore:** Once you have a basic understanding of AI, it is important to explore its potential applications in your specific area of testing. Look for ways in which AI can help you automate tasks, identify patterns and

anomalies, and improve the accuracy and speed of testing.

3. **Experiment:** After identifying potential use cases, it is important to experiment with AI tools and platforms to determine their effectiveness and suitability for your testing needs. This may involve setting up test environments, defining test scenarios, and evaluating the performance of AI-based testing approaches.

4. **Collaborate:** Collaboration with other professionals in the industry is also important. Attend conferences, join online communities, and participate in forums to learn from and collaborate with others who are also exploring AI testing.

5. **Stay current:** Finally, staying current with developments in AI and testing is crucial. Keep up with new tools, techniques, and emerging trends in AI testing to remain at the forefront of this rapidly evolving field.

6

COMMON TYPES OF SOFTWARE TESTING TECHNIQUES— FUNCTIONAL TESTING

Just like there are several common types of software testing, there are even more common types of software testing techniques that go beyond the usual testing most people know about. In this chapter, we are going to focus on a category of testing called **functional testing**. Functional testing is "a type of testing that seeks to establish whether each application feature works as per the software requirements. Each function is compared to the corresponding requirement to ascertain whether its output is consistent with the end user's expectations" (*What Is Functional Testing? Types & Examples*, n.d.). The objective of carrying out functional testing is to ensure that the system or application performs as expected and that user requirements are met.

In this case, you will be testing **how** the software works rather than its quality or performance. It will focus on the ability the user has to manage the software, if the requests are fulfilled, and if the mechanics of the application are working properly. This means, for example, that if the links to the software work, independent of the time it will take for the request to be processed. In this testing phase, different scenarios will be given to the tester, and they will carry out an investigation to ensure that the software is **usable**.

Let's take a look at the most common and important functional testing types and what they entail.

UNIT TESTING

When you think about functional testing, one of the crucial tests that needs to be carried out is called **unit testing**. This is a crucial component of the development process that helps ensure the reliability and functionality of individual code units. When I mention code units, I refer to the pieces of code that compose the software that is being developed. These smaller pieces are called "units," and, therefore, you will be testing the different parts of the code to ensure that each unit does what it is supposed to do.

Considering unit testing and keeping this example for a few other situations we will see in this chapter, you can think about a forest. When you carry out unit testing, you will be looking at specific branches of a particular tree and the leaves that compose them. In this case, to analyze the situation, you will be looking at the part that each of the leaves and branches plays in the life of the tree and if they are correctly developing, for example. In this case, this analysis will be similar to unit testing.

When a tester carries out this type of test, their main objective is to catch errors early in the development process. Most of the time, these tests are automated by the developers during coding so that they can be run multiple times to ensure that there is no problem with the code. The structure of unit tests can vary depending on the programming language and testing framework being used, but they generally follow a similar format. To carry out these actions, a setup will be done, and all the objects and dependencies will be created or initialized with different inputs to ensure that the test works under different circumstances. Based on the distinct actions that the tester asks the program to perform, they will be able to log the behavior and the output for each case.

Since I have mentioned that these tests are usually automatic and made by the developers during the coding phase, you might be asking yourself: *But who is responsible for carrying out these tests? The tester? The developer?* Well, these are very good questions. Ideally, unit tests should be created by the developers, as they have the most knowledge of the code they've written and the expected behavior. They are also in the best position to create tests that can effectively catch and prevent issues in the code.

However, in some cases, when the tester has knowledge of coding, it might be interesting to have a separate quality assurance professional test these just to make sure that the logic is correct. Furthermore, in some organizations, these tasks are separated due to the workload of the developer and the timeframe of each project. At the end of the day, it will be of the utmost importance that there is collaboration between the tester and the developer so that all the issues can be addressed and the potential problems identified and resolved.

Finally, when unit tests are carried out, they enable the possibility of saving time and money by catching defects early in the process and allowing the developer to improve the quality of the code they are using for the software or application. It is an essential part of the testing process when you consider the development of new software and will help the program be more bug-free. However, testing single lines of code and functionality is not the only essential part of testing. Read on to find out about when you look at a "part" of the program, also known as component testing.

COMPONENT TESTING

Remember how I mentioned that when you consider unit testing, you are looking at the individual branches and leaves of each tree in the forest? Well, by using the same analogy as before, I can say that **component** (or module) testing is the same as looking at the entire tree. You are still not looking at the forest as a whole and all its characteristics, but you are going to look at how each tree fits into that environment.

When this testing is conducted, you are looking at two different aspects of the software or application. The first is how each part operates individually, or isolated. The second is how these individual parts work in relation to the full program. Because it can be tested both ways, these tests are usually automated and carried out by developers once a certain module is finished. However, just like unit testing, a separate QA team can be assigned to do this if they can understand the code that was written.

Component testing is important, especially to ensure that these modules are integrated into the system with the fewest possible bugs. Since a significant system is rarely developed by only one person but rather by a development team, they need to ensure that each of their parts works before putting it together. This will ensure that bug detection is fast and avoid potential costs later in the integration phase, where it will be harder to find where the problem is located since all the modules will have been placed together.

Because of its characteristics, component testing is usually carried out after unit testing and prior to integration testing, which I will talk about next. Due to this constriction, the timing of component testing needs to be accurate: It should not be carried out too soon, before the complete module is ready, nor too late, after all parts of the program have already been put together.

Therefore, it is essential that the tester be updated by the development team on the progress of the work so that they can avoid unnecessary costs for the company. Furthermore, you must consider that looking at each of these components individually makes it easier to maintain and manage the system since it is easier to fix a smaller part than a whole system that is ready.

When you carry out component testing, there are several techniques that can be used. These include testing simulations of how components will work, known as stub testing, testing the state changes of the component, named state transition testing, and others such as mock testing, contract testing, and driver testing. It will depend on the objective of the test and what the tester wants to look at to decide what is the best option for that module of the system.

After this is done and all the components are ready to be put together, the next logical phase of testing is called integration testing.

INTEGRATION TESTING

Now, according to our tree analogy, we have looked at the branches and the trees. It is now time to see how these trees integrate into the forest as a whole. When you look at how each part of a system works together in one system, you are doing something called **integration testing**. This is the next critical part of software testing since, if the components work individually but do not work together as a whole, we can say that you have a problem.

The main purpose of carrying out this testing is to see if the units and modules are compatible with each other and that they make the system work with the fewest bugs possible. Because of this, it is important that the unit and component testing be carried out first and in an efficient manner so that when the integration part starts, the developers and the testers can be confident that it is a matter of how these work together, not that there is an individual bug elsewhere. It is in this phase that all the parts should work together like a well-oiled machine and that the system meets the requirements established by the client.

There are several ways to carry out this type of testing, and the main one is the process of adding in the components one at a time to see if there are any bugs and if the information has the correct flow between them, also known as functional incremental testing. When you consider this approach, it will be easier to add each piece at a time rather than adding them all at once and not being able to identify where the problem is coming from. In any case, some companies do prefer this approach, also known as the "big bang," which is ideal for smaller systems.

For programs or applications that contain more components, you can consider the top-down or bottom-up approaches, where the higher level or lower level components are tested first, respectively, and the other components are added later. In other cases, there might be a mixture of these approaches, which is known as a hybrid. It will all depend on the time that the team has to test the software and the deadlines and personnel available to carry out the required QA.

When you carry out integration tests (and there are professionals who are exclusively dedicated to preparing this integration phase), it is important to review as many processes as possible since any delay or bug that can be found might present a cost-related threat to the company. For example, having two components tested to see how they work together and identifying that they do not "match" might present a problem since a solution will need to be found to establish compatibility, or one of them will have to go back to the development team to be redone.

By following this process, you are able to ensure that the product is as close as possible to the client's requirements and that the system as a whole works. This will reduce the risk of errors and the generation of unnecessary costs for the organization. It will be up to the professional who is carrying out this test to ensure that the system works. This will give the team and the client confidence that the development process is going according to plan.

During this phase, they will identify each of the components of the system, establish a plan to carry out the tests, determine the order in which these same components should be placed together by creating a plan, test the system, analyze the results, and retest and inform the results if necessary. These processes consist of either a blend of manual testing and automated testing or just manual testing. It is essential that the tester have a clear idea of what the client requires to ensure that the results meet expectations.

API TESTING

When developing software, there is usually a component that is called an application programming interface, or API. If you do not know what this means, think about a connector that enables each of the components of the software to communicate. They are the "bridge" that will make each of the system parts connect to each other and share information, and because of the importance of this communication, it is essential that they are tested before releasing the software to the client. This process is known as **API testing**. One of the main characteristics that will be evaluated during this process is how the API allows the system to perform.

Imagine that in a house you have a plumbing system that enables water to flow from one room to the next. These tubes are all connected by a connector that will join them and ensure that the water flow has no interference. Now, suppose that there is a clot in one of the tubes that prevents the water from flowing appropriately. This might mean there is a problem that is preventing connections from being made. This is why testing the API is so important. By analyzing how it works and if there are any mistakes in the code, you will be able to establish if there is anything that can be done to make the software or application better.

I think that by now it is not necessary to tell you how carrying out tests will help the organization save costs because they will pick up bugs early in the process and avoid having to fix issues when the team is closer to a delivery deadline. However, there is an aspect of the API testing that needs to be considered: It is usually carried out automatically and not manually so that all the components of the program that need to be tested are tested accordingly—just like letting the water run through the pipes. Finally, consider that once you have an API that works efficiently, you will be able to use it in other projects, improving security since it has already been tested and approved and allowing reusability, saving costs and time in the next opportunity when it is used.

SYSTEM TESTING

After everything has been put together and the system is created, it is essential that **software testing** be carried out so that the full program can be evaluated. It is in this phase that the tester will see how the system works, if the integrations are running smoothly, if it can perform in the designated final environment, and if it is ready to be used by the final client. Because of these characteristics, this phase consists of a comprehensive test that will evaluate not only the software itself but also how it interacts with the hardware, other software, the company's network, the internet (in the case of online-run programs), and any other feature that might affect how it works.

The main difference from the previous kinds of testing we have seen is that the tester will not be looking at each part individually but rather at its operation as a whole when it is placed in a real-world scenario. The tester will look at items such as the scalability of the program, or how much it can grow to have new users, its performance, if it is compatible with other programs, if there is any overload when it is working in these scenarios leading to crashes and problems, and, of course, if the system is reliable and safe to be implemented and used by the client.

Although we could say that all of the testing that we are looking at in this book is, in some way, a system test, I wanted to place this here in the functionality testing chapter because it is, in a certain way, one of the testing types that can be carried out. For example, companies that are developing smaller systems might test everything at once because the cost that would be incurred from testing the software per part would be more costly than doing it all at once because of its size. However, even after this process is carried out, there is still one final test we must consider that will evaluate how the system works as a whole, and this will be how the client analyzes it, also known as acceptance testing.

ACCEPTANCE TESTING

When the system has been thoroughly tested by the QA team and they are sure that every part of it is as bug-free as possible, it is time to check if the final product meets clients' expectations. This testing is called **acceptance testing** and will match what has been done by the development team to the client's requirements, demands, and expectations. It is usually the last part of the process. During this phase, a representative from the client might be invited to test the system out prior to its deployment to all the other users so they can provide feedback and let the team know if the expectations are met.

Meeting the user requirements is the main part of the program development process, since it will be they who will manage the system and who need to be satisfied with the result. This means that the user will need to validate all the functionalities and the usability of the software to ensure that it is according to what was established in the initial meetings when the demands were taken note of. Sometimes, although acceptance testing is the last part of the process, it can be done in different parts of the system and at different moments to ensure that the progress is satisfactory.

If the final user or client is not satisfied with the final result of the program, this can mean that there will be more costs and that some parts might need to be done again. For this reason, it is essential that the tester be present in the requirements meeting when the client determines what they want their system to be like, so that they can ensure that the process is going according to plan. In addition to this, the tester should always accompany or shadow the client when performing the tests to take notes on any important observations, bugs that are identified, and changes that might be made.

Apart from this, if the tester is present during the final validation, they will be able to ensure that the process is carried out correctly and completely and that all the necessary items have been validated. While these tests are being carried out, it is essential that the client, tester, and development team maintain open communication and that all parties are involved to avoid potential misunderstandings. Furthermore, it will be of the utmost importance that this process be documented and approved by all parties to ensure that there are no problems with potential variations in the future where the client claims they said they wanted something that was not done.

This is one of the parts of the process that takes the most time for different reasons, and it is essential that the process is not rushed. The user needs to take their time to ensure that they understand the flow and that everything they want is there. Even if a minor problem is found, a note should be made and the issue addressed prior to releasing the final version. Finally, giving the tester an adequate amount of time to carry out the process will enable potential bugs or flow problems to be identified, bringing more confidence to the final product.

END-TO-END TESTING

Remember when you test a system for APIs you can think about the water tubes in a house? Well, I am going to use this same example for **end-to-end (E2E) testing**. When you carry out a test like this, it means that you are going to test it from start to finish, much like identifying if the water flowing into and out of the house is working. This testing will look at the program or application from start to finish to ensure that the whole system is working appropriately. In this case, the test will simulate real-life use and application as if the user were accessing the system.

During this process, the environment will be set up on a machine to simulate the conditions in which the user will access the program for the tests to be executed. This will be carried out by the tester to ensure that all the client requirements are met. However, once again, I want to reinforce that the tester will not just be "clicking away." This process is carried out in a planned and systematic way to ensure that all the potential issues are identified and that all scenarios are tested accordingly. Once the tests are concluded, the results will be analyzed to identify if the software is compliant.

Although there are different ways to approach this process, one of the ways that testers can identify if the program is in accordance with the standards is by establishing metrics that will enable them to quantify the results. These metrics can include how long each test takes to be executed, if there are any overload or stability problems when the program is running, and even the success rating of the process. Because these tests are so comprehensive and complex, they might take some time to be executed and, therefore, must be planned accordingly so that no delays are incurred for the delivery of the final product.

One of the main advantages of this test is that, since it will be applied on a real-life basis, any potential bugs that might have been missed during the other test phases can be identified and corrected. It will also be important to foresee during this process any "deviations" or unexpected actions in the actions conducted by the user while they are working with the software. This will be the last step of testing prior to deploying the application to the final user, and, therefore, you should consider that it is the "final barrier" between the development and the release phase.

OTHER FUNCTIONALITY TESTS

Now that we have seen some of the major functionality tests that can be carried out—from unit to E2E testing—I want to rewind a little and mention a few other tests that can also be carried out for functionality appraisal but were not yet mentioned. However, this is not because they are less common or important—because they are. But these tests are more specific and are used in certain situations in which the testers have more time to execute them. In addition to this, these other tests can be executed together with the tests in the other phases and could be considered a "component" of them or a "special action." Let's take a look at what these are, how they can be applied, and the importance of carrying them out.

Smoke Testing

When you think about a program or a system, you might know that there are critical elements that are part of it. For example, for payment software, receiving confirmation that the payment has gone through is considered essential, as well as an agenda for a patient to see what the available times are for a doctor's appointment. These are the **core** features of a program that will be tested in a process known as **smoke testing**.

These tests are usually not long and comprehensive, but rather short, shallow, and fast since their main objective is to ensure that a determined functionality is working according to expectations. This is the first step that is carried out before a deeper analysis is carried out because it will enable the tester to see if there are any issues that will prevent them from performing other tests. It is safe to say, when you consider a smoke test, that it will ensure that the major functionalities of the program have a basic level of performance to ensure that the rest of the system can be tested.

Usually, if an application's main features pass the smoke test, the tester is allowed to continue with other tests. Think about it this way: What is the use of having software that works if the user cannot log in to the page? Therefore, ensuring that basic features can be accomplished will move the program into the next phase of testing. The importance of this test is that it will save time and money for the company. Once again, if the basic and essential features do not work, there is no reason to keep developing until they do.

Most of the time, these tests are run through automated tools to ensure that they are accurate. Sometimes, the tester will add certain triggers that will request one action or another to see how the system will respond. Since the basic features of software are usually simple actions that are essential for it to work, it does not require a human to carry out the test, only to monitor it. In addition to this, when you add automation to smoke tests, it will enable you to update them to reflect the changes as they are done, saving labor time for the tester.

Looking at the bigger picture, you will see that these tests will help save time and money for the company. But what is even more important is that they will help ensure that the development team maintains a good reputation for being efficient and thorough during their process. These may seem like "basic" tests, but they are in reality one of the most important steps to ensuring software functionality in the early development stage.

Sanity Testing

Much like smoke testing, when a **sanity test** is carried out, it is meant to be fast and efficient. These are usually carried out to confirm that a change made in the code still maintains functionality or a certain feature. This will be done to establish if there is enough stability in the program to ensure that it can continue running and for other features to be tested. Because of its characteristics, it is usually carried out **after** the smoke test and **before** the regression testing, which we will see in the following section of this chapter.

When you think about this type of testing, I want you to consider it as "checking the check," where the tester looks to see if the previous bugs that were reported have been corrected and that further testing is possible. Let's go back to the tubing in the house example. Suppose that you ran the water and identified the clot. Once this was done, you fixed it. The next step will be to run the water again and see if it is now flowing correctly throughout the house. This action of running the water again is what sanity testing is.

Some of the advantages of sanity testing include the identification of problems that can lead to other issues in the software development process and the identification of pieces of code and information that might be missing. It also provides quick feedback on an issue and a fast response to a bug when it is required. Because of its simplicity and lack of structured reporting, it is fast and generally inexpensive compared to the costs that can be incurred by finding bugs throughout the development process.

While this testing presents several advantages, such as looking into specific features and being able to address them quickly, it also has some disadvantages that must be considered. One of the major problems is giving the tester the false feeling that everything is working according to plan. Since sanity testing by default only looks at a certain part of the software, this might prevent the tester from seeing how it affects the program on a larger scale. This means that a change in the code could have worked for a specific feature but that it has created bugs in others.

If you also consider that these tests are very specific, carrying out sanity tests in all the applications of the software is something impossible that can become very time-consuming and costly if it is a requirement. These tests are made to be quick, which can lead to limitations in the evaluation, such as incomplete testing because you are not looking at the full picture. If time is a critical factor in the development and deployment of this software, you could face a problem if many sanity tests are required.

Due to its limited characteristics, I would not recommend having sanity testing be the only testing process that you carry out. It should be part of a larger testing process that will evaluate all the features of the program. We will look at one of these tests now, known as regression testing.

Regression Testing

Regression testing can be carried out during any phase of the software development process: unit, component, API, or regression testing. The main reason for this is that this test should be carried out periodically to ensure that the code you are using is effective for the program you are developing. When you carry out regression testing, it is a way of checking that what was previously done is not impacted by the new features that were created for the program. This essentially means checking that the new code does not negatively impact or create a bug for something that already existed and was tested.

This is a sort of cumulative testing, much like working on an electrical panel in your home. You will first check the energy availability in the region. Then you will run all the wiring and test it to ensure that there is no fire risk. Next, you will install all the energy outputs and test them to ensure that there are no problems. You will carry out the power testing in the house step by step to be sure that there are no hazards, and you will cumulatively check each of them with the electrical panel before putting them all to work at once.

Think of each part of the house as a different part of the system. Just as you are checking as you build and make connections, the same is being done with software. You are making sure that the next steps do not negatively impact the previous features and that everything is working seamlessly. Much like a home, if you do not carry out a regression test, it is impossible to determine if everything in your software is working correctly according to the specifications and that the upgrades that are made are efficient.

Regression tests can be either manual or automated, and the use of either one will usually depend on the budget and time that you have available. For example, creating an automation framework that will continuously be updated to match the system requirements can be costly and time-consuming, much like creating a different piece of software in itself. Some development teams might not have the budget to do this, and the most cost-effective manner would be to carry out these tests manually. In addition to this, building or using automation tools will require constant maintenance since they will need to be updated to match current software standards. When you consider the approach you will take to carrying out these tests, it will be essential to look at the pros and cons of each alternative and the resources that you have available to do so.

White Box Testing

You might have noticed that, so far, I haven't talked about the testing of the code itself. Well, that was until now. When a professional carries out **white box testing**, they are literally looking into the code, its logic, flow, and interactions in the back end of a system. This can be done to a unit, a component, or the full system, depending on which stage of development the software is in. The main reason why developers carry out these tests is to ensure that there is correct integration in the code and that there is an understandable logic to it.

Needless to say, the professionals who work with this type of testing need to understand about code. Much like the difference between a clinic doctor and a surgeon, these testers need to be able to know how to understand and "read" the inner workings of the system to assess if everything is functioning correctly. Because of this, this type of test is also known as structural or code-based testing, since it will analyze the core of the program and how the code is enabling it to perform.

Some of the main functions of a system will be analyzed when this is carried out, including security features, error handling, and performance, as well as whether all the code is being effectively used, there is no "useless code," and the code is as succinct and optimal as necessary to make the system work. This means that although developers have different ways of addressing a certain issue, sometimes they can use more code lines than necessary to make a statement that could be done with fewer lines.

Although most of the process will be the same as the other testing types, by identifying and establishing test cases, writing, executing, and analyzing the tests, there is a step to be taken prior to this, which is when the tester will have to understand the code and what the developers have done. Independently of the language that has been used, the tester will need the appropriate knowledge to ensure that they can apply the best practices and cover as much information as possible.

Black Box Testing

Contrary to white box testing, when a tester carries out black box testing, they are testing the software without looking specifically into the code. This is the most common type of testing, which can be carried out by several of the parties involved in the program's development—from the developer to the QA team. When this test is carried out, you can think of it as being similar to an airplane black box. It will see the input that the user gives and the output that will come from it, but the processes in the middle will not be considered.

By doing this, the basic functionalities of the program can be tested, but especially the view that the user will have of the program since there is no need to know how its "inside" works. "Just like end-users 'don't care' how a system is coded or architected and expect to receive an appropriate response to their requests, a tester can simulate user activity and see if the system delivers on its promises" (Imperva, n.d.). In this fast-approached test, the tester needs to be free of any preliminary views they might have of the program. On the other hand, this view can be somewhat limiting since if there is a bug, the reason **why** it is having a problem will not be seen by the tester.

In addition to this, black box testing will focus **exclusively** on the functional requirements of the system, leaving to the side anything that might be non-functional, possibly creating gaps within the process. However, this is a perfect opportunity for testers that are beginning their careers to learn some of the testing basics and for other testers that do not know coding.

When carrying out a black box test, the professional can choose several different techniques to do so. They can separate the system into "groups," where they will input the information on one end and see the output on the other, also known as equivalence partitioning. Another approach is called "error guessing," where the tester will test for the most common mistakes that developers make when building software and target these areas. Sometimes, these tests can be carried out together with "exploratory testing," in which, as the name suggests, the tester will explore different functionalities of the program that might not be specifically covered in the other tests that were carried out by the program.

While this can be considered a comprehensive test technique that can additionally analyze how the software transitions from one phase to the next and identify the program's different behaviors, it also has its limitations because of the lack of depth it presents. It might be an interesting way to proceed with testing at a surface level, but it must be placed together with other tests, especially those that analyze non-functional features that the program may have. On the other hand, we will now see something that can be considered the "middle way" between white and black box testing. Can you guess what it is? If you said "grey box" testing, then you are correct! Let's take a look to see what it consists of.

Grey Box Testing

Grey box testing, as the name might suggest, happens when the tester mixes black and white box testing to come up with a hybrid and more comprehensive solution. This means that while they will only look at the inputs and outputs of the system, they will do so with knowledge of the code and the program's inner workings. However, this is usually not done to the whole system because it would take too much time and the costs would be considerable. In these cases, specific and targeted parts of the software are selected to be tested, especially those that are the most critical and may present a vulnerability or a defect that can affect the user experience.

Some benefits of using the grey box technique, according to *Grey Box Testing* (n.d.-a) include:

- the combination of the best characteristics of black and white box testing
- testing performed according to the user's needs and requirements
- more quality of the tests that are carried out and more comprehensive results
- more efficient and faster
- the ability to quickly fix identified bugs
- input from all the involved parties in the software development

However, you might be asking yourself, *What are the white and black box characteristics that this test includes? If this testing has the best of both tools, why not just use it?* Well, those are very good questions to be asked. Good for you for thinking about them, because they really make a lot of sense.

The thing is that grey box testing also has its limitations, such as finding someone within the testing team that has the code knowledge to evaluate the software. In addition to this, if you consider that the grey box testing is limited and targets specific parts of the software, this may mean that other parts are left out. Or maybe even a part of the code might not be addressed simply because it is not part of the requirements or the tester does not have enough knowledge to comment on the changes that need to be made. Therefore, while it may be simpler than carrying out a white box test or more detailed than a black box test, companies need to consider the necessity of adding other tests to this phase to ensure that the full system is analyzed and that a complete integration analysis is carried out.

Finally, when you consider grey box testing, you might want to think of some of the methods that can be associated with it, such as, for example, regression testing, which we have already seen. These tests are considered great to be performed when you are dealing with web or smaller applications that are more simple. In addition to this, by carrying out grey box testing, it is possible to look at the system's main functionalities and code without getting too deep into its inner workings.

Interface Testing

Consider a website. Imagine that it needs to be able to run on several different browsers on different devices and be available both online and offline. In addition to this, if your software is being used by an external company, they are likely using their own network and server, and you will need to test how they work within your company's structure. All of these items are verified during what is known as **interface testing**. "When an application or software or a website is developed, then there are several components of it. Those components can be a server, database, etc. The connection which integrates and facilitates the communication between these components is termed an interface" (*What Is Interface Testing? Know Its Types, Strategy and Tools*, 2023).

When these tests are carried out, they have the objective of identifying whether the communication between the different parts of the system is working in the correct manner. This means communicating with other software that might be used, with the internet, with the server, and with the hardware, among others. If you think this sounds like an integration test, then you are correct! However, while the integration testing will look at how the different components of the system will interact with each other, the interface testing will look at how these integrate with applications that are external to the software.

To do this, the tester must identify all the parts that the program will interact with and which ones need to be taken into consideration during the testing phase. After this, the process is similar to what we have seen: define, develop, execute, analyze, fix errors, and repeat to ensure that everything is correct. If you consider the different types of languages and technologies that exist, you will see that this type of testing is crucial to ensuring that communication is not hindered for any reason.

As we have seen, these can include compatibility testing with different browsers, the graphic interface that the user will see when they access the program, if the system is able to navigate easily, and if the APIs are properly working. By looking at the functionality of the programs, this will reduce any losses that might occur or any potential bugs that might appear when accessing the program from different places.

7

COMMON TYPES OF SOFTWARE TESTING TECHNIQUES—NON-FUNCTIONAL TESTING

I f functional testing means that the usability of the system is being tested, then I could say that non-functional testing includes everything but. One example of this situation is security testing. Whether a system is secure or not may not influence how the user will manage the system, but it is nonetheless important to ensure that the company's other systems and applications are protected from malicious invasions. Other tests include performance, network, and stress tests, all of which we will now see.

In this chapter, we are going to look at 23 different types of non-functional tests that a developer can carry out and the importance each one of them has during the SDLC. As you read, you will be able to understand that these tests are performed to help increase usability, maintainability, and reduce risks during production—all of which, in the end, will help reduce costs for the organization that is developing and for the client. Much like functional testing, requesting non-functional tests as part of the strategy for developing software will be essential to ensuring the quality of the final product.

COMPATIBILITY TESTING

Have you ever, while using your computer or mobile phone, received the message that "This program is not compatible with the version of the program you are using"? If you have, then you will understand the need for **compatibility testing**. This test happens when you see if the software you are developing is compatible with the different browsers, hardware, operational systems, and any other components necessary to run tests. This means that the program will be tested in different environments to ensure that it works properly in the largest variety possible so that it can reach as many users as possible, especially in the case of web applications, thus ensuring a larger market share.

When compatibility is not tested, this can lead to a bad user experience and increase the number of complaints that a company might receive. Another example of a reason to test compatibility is to recommend to the user the best way to use the software. For example, when you see the message "This program works better with [insert here the name of a browser, for example]," this means that it has been tested and the best results presented were those when this specific browser was used. Another simple and common example is when you open a web page on your computer browser, but it does not perform the same when you open it on your mobile. This means that it has not been made compatible with a mobile version.

Compatibility testing is usually planned, and the tester will make a list of all the applications, devices, platforms, and operational systems that they want to target-test the software on. Next, they will prepare the environment, although there are several tools today that enable you to carry out the testing without having to set up the environment yourself. These tools include BrowserStack, TestingBot, BrowseEmALL, and LambdaTest, to name a few (*Compatibility Testing*, n.d.).

However, if you decide to carry out the testing yourself, you will next need to prepare each of the test cases to ensure that all of the possibilities are covered within the desired scope. The tester will then execute the tests according to the list and plan they have developed, and as soon as this is done, the results will be analyzed. If there are any corrections to be made, they will be passed on to the development team and restarted once the issues have been addressed.

Apart from the testing on each platform with intended use, the tester can run two different types of compatibility testing known as **backward compatibility** and **forward compatibility**. The idea of each one is rather simple and easy to understand if you relate the tests to their names. In the backward compatibility testing, the professional will test if the software is compatible with certain **previous** versions of browsers, hardware, and operating systems.

It is an important part of the testing procedure to ensure that users who have not updated their systems will still be able to use the program. Consider, for example, when you have software that is upgraded. It needs to be compatible with previous versions of an operating system, for example, to ensure that users won't lose their data or suffer crashes while they are using it.

On the other hand, I guess you might already imagine what forward compatibility is. In this case, it will consist of testing the developed software with the **newer** versions of the same applications. This means that the application is able to run in newer and possibly more modern versions of a browser, for example, without presenting any bugs. This might happen when the company does not feel the need to immediately update the software to match the latest version of the application, but it will still work if the user decides to upgrade, for example.

MAINTAINABILITY TESTING

Suppose a client has requested that your company develop software for them. However, one of their demands is that it be easy to maintain by their own IT team, including that the documentation be complete and that they can modify it without further trouble if needed. This means that you will likely have to run a **maintainability testing** session to ensure that this is possible. In other words, this type of testing will determine how easy it is to keep the application running smoothly after it has been deployed.

When the tester is carrying out this type of test, they will need to look at specific points that will help them determine if the software is easily maintainable or not. These include

- **Scalability:** The tester should certify that it is possible to upscale or downscale the system easily without changing too much of the code. This means it should be able to handle an increase in users without compromising its performance abilities and remain efficient for the client if there is a growing amount of data or traffic in the software. In these cases, the software should keep being reliable and safe under these circumstances and guarantee that minor changes, if any, are needed to support the increase in demand.

- **Readability (code quality):** When you consider code quality, this means that the code is easy to read, with comments where needed, and that only necessary lines of code are used in the program. This increases the chances of others understanding what the developer meant and changing the code if it comes to it. The code should be written in such a way that it is concise and easy to understand, with no "polluting" comments, and in compliance with industry standards and conventions to ensure that it is understood by everyone.

- **Documentation:** Even though some developers do not like to write documentation, it is a necessary part of ensuring the maintainability of the software. This means that the tester will need to check if it is complete and covers all aspects of the program that is being developed. The documentation should match the code and be up-to-date with any changes that are made during the correction processes, for example. Instructions on how to implement the program and how the system works will be essential to ensuring that the system is easily maintainable.

- **Modularity:** When software that has several features is being created, the development team must ensure that it is done so in modules to ensure that if one part is changed, it will not significantly affect the whole program. This means that it should be easy to separate, making it easier to maintain. This principle should be checked by the tester, which will help ensure that changes are easy to carry out, that the software is maintainable and updateable by parts, and that the impacts are reduced in the rest of the system when these actions are carried out.

- **Compatibility:** Since we have seen this type of testing and what it entails in the previous section, I will just do a small recap. When the tester ensures compatibility, it means that the system should be compatible with a variety of platforms, devices, and software versions, allowing for easy updates and maintenance.

- **Extensibility:** The last requisite that needs to be observed during maintainability testing is similar to scalability, since it talks about an augmentation in the system. However, in this case, we are not talking about the increase in the number of users or data, but in the number of features and functionalities that will be added. Being able to do this with another team, if necessary, will be important, and, therefore, everything should be prepared for this to take place.

Finally, you must consider that since the software is "live" during the SDLC, it will be essential to carry out maintainability testing as each of its modules is ready. By evaluating it in parts, this will make the tester's job more efficient and enable them to identify more issues since they will not have to focus on the full system but rather analyze it in parts.

COMPLIANCE TESTING

Compliance testing is carried out to ensure that the software is in accordance with the regulatory and contractual requirements that were established by the client and that the industry rules, guidelines, and standards are followed. In addition to this, in some cases, it might be subject to certain laws according to the country in which it will be deployed and must comply with governmental determinations. One of the main reasons to have compliant software is so that there are no regulatory problems that may lead to liabilities, sanctions, or legal actions because of its characteristics.

Sometimes companies might want to invest in the ISO certification for the software, with which they will undergo an audit to be accredited under ISO 27001, which is for certification in meeting requirements for an information security management system. Other certifications that can be applied include:

- HIPAA compliance, which will protect patients' information in medical systems
- EU data protection regulation, which complies with the European Union's readiness
- compliance with GDPR principles laid out in ISO 9001:2015 for quality management systems
- ISO 13485, which is a certification that was designed for the production, design, and installation of medical devices and similar services

Because some software might have a global reach (which we will see in a little bit), it is important that the tester has knowledge about these rules and regulations. Furthermore, the process might be lengthy and demanding since the rules may change and specific criteria need to be met according to the software's characteristics. In some cases, the company might want to involve the legal or compliance departments while this test is being carried out to ensure that all requirements are met.

USABILITY TESTING

As the name might suggest, **usability testing** is a test that is carried out by the user with a tester to see how they manage the software and if there are any areas that can be improved. However, this test is different from acceptance testing, which we have seen before, because it will not look for any bugs and is not a focus group, where the users will talk about what they like and dislike about the program and how each one interacts with it individually.

This is the only type of test that comes to mind when thinking about a testing method that does not necessarily need to be carried out by professionals. This is because any individual with experience in research, design, or user experience can do them and report the results. However, because this test can be carried out by a non-technical tester, other research and testing techniques should be considered throughout the process to ensure that all bases are covered. Furthermore, since this involves the way the user interacts with the system, it will be essential that it be carried out continuously to ensure that the feedback is constant.

Some companies will have user experience (UX) professionals that will help developers in this stage, while others might ask the client to provide feedback. The important thing in this phase is that any usability issues can be found early in the process before more of the application is developed, ensuring that there are no wasted efforts or resources. When the intended audience reacts positively to its characteristics and considers it user-friendly, the developers will be able to move on and continue the coding process.

This testing can be carried out on the user interface, the content, the navigation, and other elements that might be considered important by the team. If this test is carried out correctly, it can reduce negative experiences from the users and potentially negative feedback, ensuring that a costly reformulation, for example, will be necessary and that it is likely more people will use it. Usability testing can also be advantageous by helping to ensure that users are engaged while using it, that there are better conversion rates (for sales sites, for example), and that it has a higher reach and better ranking in search engines. At the end of the day, usability testing is all about guaranteeing that the user is satisfied with the final result and that the software delivers what is expected from it, enhancing brand reputation and enabling a positive evaluation in the market.

Failover Testing

Imagine that you are the owner of one of the largest banks in the country and, suddenly, one day, the server where you host all the company's transactions fails and nothing works anymore. You would say that it is essential that the system recover as fast as possible so that the bank is not impacted by the server failure and that customers can continue to carry out their business as usual. In this case, if you have carried out a **failover test**, you will learn how much time the systems take to recover and use an alternate server.

This is because when failover testing is performed, it aims to identify if the system can allocate information and operations to another system when there is a failure. This test will enable the client to see how fast the recovery is and protect themselves from reputational damage and financial losses, for example. This means that when this test is carried out, most of the scenarios are evaluated, such as network crashes, power outages, or security breaches. On the other hand, it will not evaluate the effects of potential disasters, for which there is a separate kind of test that we will see next. Failover testing will cover the main security issues regarding weaknesses and potential disruptions by connecting it to another server, for example, and reducing the time it will take the software to recover.

Most of the time, testers will carry out this process to ensure that the end user does not even notice the change. This means that while the owner of the software will be having problems, those who are effectively using the system will not notice because the process is so fast and unnoticeable, fulfilling the main objective of this test. In this case, the company that owns the program might have certain security features installed and ready for action, such as load balancers, clusters, and alternate server options.

By using failover clusters, for example, this will give the software an alternate direction to go if there is a failure in the primary system. This is considered essential— can you imagine what would happen to a hospital if the system failed and they could not access critical data from patients? Therefore, especially for those systems that provide critical services, it is essential that this testing be carried out. Clusters will enable the system to be available and reliable, most of the time enabling more information to be added to them if needed.

When this process of transferring to another server happens, it is called an application server failover. This means that the primary server went down and that the secondary server took over its operations to ensure that requests are correctly processed. When you consider the implications of a server failure that will disable certain programs from working correctly, this can mean money loss and potential security problems. Since user data is usually the most important part of a system—so much so that specific legislation has been and is being created for this—you will understand why this change is so important.

Finally, in addition to the failover process, there is another called **failback**, which simply means that the software is being directed back to the original server. This can be done once the primary server is fixed or the issues have been addressed. In this case, the transition also needs to be seamless and undetectable by the client to ensure a positive experience with the software. We could say that failover and failback are **complementary** services that need to be tested before software is deployed. This will usually be done in the client's environment, since this is where the software will be hosted, which can be on an on-premises server, in the cloud, or a hybrid of both. One of the things that will be essential during this phase is that **everything** that was carried out in software while it was using the secondary server is backed up and synchronized so that the primary server can maintain and retrieve the data that was added or generated while it was not being used.

Disaster Recovery Testing

Although disasters are rare, it is especially important for companies to be prepared for them. Think about when COVID-19 struck and the companies were not ready for everyone staying home and working remotely. Since then, companies have changed their risk management strategy, which includes testing their software for disaster recovery situations. Among the disasters that can be named, we could talk about natural disasters, such as snowstorms or heavy rain, significant power outages, and even cyberattacks with malicious intentions.

When you consider these disasters, it can mean that a company can suffer severe losses, from hardware to user data, which can bring severe money loss issues and repu-tational problems. Therefore, when **disaster recovery testing** is carried out, the tester will be looking at poten-tial vulnerabilities in the environment and potential recovery plans so that the company can be prepared for such events. This means being prepared, thinking about alternate solutions that can serve as a way out, and ensuring that the recovery plans are efficient and reliable.

Even though this test can be costly, think about how much more it will cost the company if they are **not** prepared to deal with it. Therefore, together with the testing, a plan should be established that will be followed in case a disaster occurs. This plan is what will be validated during the disaster recovery testing process, which can be carried out in several different ways, for example, synchronized and asynchronous. This will determine how the data is replicated to other locations in case calamity strikes.

Other methods apart from the simulation include more complete tests such as full-scale testing, where everything will be shut down and the recovery system will be tested, or a tabletop exercise, where the process will just be followed through on paper by being reviewed and discussed by all the involved parties. The second method—although it might not be the most effective way to see if the plan will effectively work when the time comes—is the least costly and is considered step one to prepare for these situations.

The most important part of the process of disaster recovery is that the documentation is updated and current with the company's current structure. To ensure this, carrying out this test periodically is essential, as is keeping it in an accessible place where others can manage it. Can you imagine if only one person knows about the plan and they are sick on the day it happens? How will the company manage? This is why it is essential to involve all the stakeholders in the process and widely communicate the actions that need to be taken across the relevant departments.

Other essential steps to have better chances of success include establishing a test environment similar to the production environment, streamlining the process by using automation tools and reducing the chance of human error (which can also be a disaster). By carrying out these processes effectively and diligently, the company will be better prepared to face potential disaster situations and avoid suffering problems that might lead to a loss of money.

Localization and Internationalization Testing

If you have ever accessed a website, for example, and received the message that "This page is not available in your region," then you might understand the impor-tance of **localization** and **internationalization testing**. While these are distinct concepts, they are closely related to each other since internationalization testing will need to verify the localization as well. When you carry out localization testing, or L10N tests, you are ensuring that the software is available in a different location or region, along with the language that will be used.

On the other hand, when you consider the levels of globalization that we have reached with the internet and the multinationality of thousands of companies, it will be essential that the software they use is standardized to ensure efficiency. Therefore, there is a need to have the software appropriately configured locally so it can later be expanded globally in a more accessible and user-friendly manner. These characteristics will be used especially when the internationalization testing, or I18N, test is carried out.

Therefore, when you consider localization, you need to think locally or regionally, and when you think about internationalization, your mind should immediately relate to the global aspect of the software. Both of these types of testing are important because they will directly impact the user experience and their satisfaction while using the software. To name an example, if you are using a data system for software that will be used both in the United States and in England, you must be able to change the view so that the information is presented according to the culture of each country, or mm/dd/yyyy for Americans and dd/mm/yyyy for English users.

To successfully carry out this testing, you will need to identify the audience for whom the software is being developed and see what the requirements are. Be sure to take into consideration all of the different nuances of the region, if it is local, or the cultures, in the case of international software. It is important to note that the different compliance requirements for different locations are met. When these characteristics are ensured, the program being developed will be accessible to more users.

PERFORMANCE TESTING

Performance testing is exactly what the name suggests: to evaluate how the software works in terms of response times, speed, and demand. This type of testing is essential when you consider testing since it will be the measured performance that will determine the experience the user has. If you have ever used a program that presented "bugs" or latency when there were too many users, you probably know what I mean. In spite of seeing these on many different systems, one of the places in which they are most common is in the gaming industry, to ensure that the game does not have a "lag" or that it does not "crash" because of the number of people playing.

If you consider that the user experience is what will drive more people to use your application, then you must ensure that it is working without any problems. The lack of users can lead to people leaving the platform and, consequently, a drop in the revenue that the program will bring. In addition to this, in the case of companies, if the system is too slow, it might demotivate users from putting it into action and generate complaints that might lead to abandoning the project in full. In other words, wasted money.

One of the main items that will be observed when a performance test is done is how well the software can handle an increase in users, or its scalability. Depending on the client's requirements, it should handle the expected number of users and also be prepared if this number grows. To make sure that the scenarios are correctly tested, it will be important that real-life data is used for both the effective number of users and also the estimated number (which might increase over time). It will be essential to create a testing environment similar to the one where the software will be deployed.

Some of these tests might be automated, since they will require the analysis of the system's response time and metrics about the resources used. I suggest that when there is a request to carry out performance tests, they be done every time a new module is added to the system to see how it affects its general effectiveness. This test can also be carried out with others, such as compatibility testing, where the performance will be evaluated according to the browser, for example, that is being used and the server characteristics.

Load Testing

Although the concept of **load testing** is one type of performance testing, when you carry out this type of test, it will focus specifically on how the system will respond when there is a lot of information being processed. This can mean that there are many people using the system, too many requests, or even too much data being transferred. The load testing will evaluate how **stable** the system is regarding this increase in demand and if it is **reliable** enough to support an increase in its workload.

One of the processes that can be carried out is that if you carry out a performance test and see that there are delays in the system, you then perform a load test to ensure that this is not the problem. By identifying potential delays in system responses, the owner of the software will face fewer problems and complaints from clients. Suppose that you have a system delay and people are complaining that there are crashes in the software. You might carry out a load test to determine if the network and the server to which the software is connected can handle the estimated workload or if the problem is with the design.

And, although this test is essential, we see the effects of not performing it quite often. Think about when you want to buy tickets to a famous singer's show. Many times, the platform that hosts the ticket sales cannot accommodate the demand that is being made and "crashes," generating numerous complaints from the clients. Some of these system failures are so famous that they have even made the news. This leads to serious damages in reputation and image for the company that administers the software. No one will blame the developer—they do not even know who that is! All they will remember is the name of the company.

The main objective of load testing is to ensure that the system will operate under different stress conditions and take its performance metrics for the "down" and the "up" times. When this is done, the tester is able to tell the client how much "stress" the software can absorb and help them make a better decision about whether to scale it or not. For this, they must have an idea of the expected number of users and test the software with this data. Much like performance testing, ensuring that the test is carried out in the correct environment with the most realistic number possible will help make design modifications or change the development strategy if necessary.

Since it would take hundreds or thousands of users to simulate a potential stress on the system, this test is usually done in an automated way with tools that are available on the market. This way, a computer can be told what load should be applied, so the testing can be more effective. This will also enable the tester to create different scenarios according to the plan they have established and effectively measure the test results.

Scalability Testing

While it might be easy because of the scope that it presents, you should not confuse load testing, which we have just seen, with **scalability testing**. The main difference between both of them is that while load testing will be carried out on a larger scale and is mostly automated, enabling the identification of rare or hard-to-catch bugs, scalability testing will run the software through different perspectives and configurations to see how it behaves according to how much is demanded from it (RedLine13, 2017). We could maybe say that scalability testing is the more targeted version of load testing.

When a scalability test is run, it can be done to see the behavior of the software if there is an increase or decrease in a specific metric. Although it will likely not reach the stress level, which we will see next, the idea is to see what its capacity is. Six specific items are looked at when you consider scalability testing. They are (*Scalability Testing*, n.d.):

- throughput
- performance
- memory usage
- CPU usage
- network usage
- response time

Among the benefits of carrying out scalability tests are the possibility of identifying potential changes to be made in the software and the identification of problems prior to deployment. When the software is tested under the correct circumstances and using the correct environment, it will enable the tester to have an accurate vision of how the system performs under different conditions. Two other benefits include saving money by not having to correct mistakes and avoiding losing money due to reputation problems or bad user experiences.

Therefore, even if it is only one of the tests that the company intends to carry out, it should be considered an essential item in the SDLC development strategy. This test will ensure that your software is reliable and that the customer will not have problems, even in peak seasons. Imagine when the holiday season comes and there are thousands of customers shopping for their gifts online. If a scalability test is not performed, it might lead the company to not take preventive measures during this part of the year to ensure that everyone has a good experience.

On the other hand, there are also several issues with carrying out this type of test, especially when the customer's use and environment cannot be replicated by the tester to adequately verify the metrics. It is also a test that can take some time because of the different perspectives that have to be looked at, and if the time is limited to carry them out, they might not be done in full or appropriately, or might even cause a delay in the deployment phase. Therefore, an alternative to this test is what we will see next, which is to identify the breaking point of the software load, or stress testing.

Stress Testing (Breaking Point)

Stress testing means that the tester will make the software undergo extreme overload situations to see when it will fail. For this reason, it is also known as a "breaking point test," where the system will be forced to work under stress conditions until there is a problem with performance or in its functionalities. The main idea here is to be able to prevent the system from failing when these conditions occur and be able to plan a strategy if it does.

I remember during the pandemic, when everybody was locked at home and everyone was doing their grocery shopping online, something curious caught my attention. Many local stores, which were not used to dealing with so many online requests, were constantly crashing because of the demand—the system had obviously reached its stress point. However, with everything as unpredictable as it was, they came up with a simple solution that momentarily solved the problem until it could be looked deeper into.

They came up with a queue system where the customer would "wait" in a virtual queue until it was their time to carry out their shopping. Since this was a constant demand, when the system would become too "stressed," they would activate this protocol to ensure that there were no crashes in the system and that all clients had the opportunity to carry out their shopping. If there is one thing I am certain many companies have learned from this experience, it is the need to perform this test in case of emergencies.

The test is carried out similarly to other tests. The developer prepares the test scenario and the environment, and by automating testing, they overload the software with information. In this case, there should be someone monitoring the system and applying increasing levels of load to measure when it will effectively fail. You should also determine the metrics that will be monitored, such as memory use.

By fixing this problem or finding alternatives to it early in the software development phases, the company will be able to avoid having problems due to delayed responses when there is too much demand. This could mean having a simple alternative like the one I mentioned or any other strategy that the development team might find together with the customer. However, it is essential that this point be identified so that while the program is operating and being monitored, the breaking point can be foreseen.

Here, the essential word is **strategy**, since most companies today have an online presence. With the competition available in the market, it is likely that if the system does not correspond to the user's expectations, they might migrate to another place to do their shopping, leading to a loss of revenue. Take into consideration that for software that is essential for a company's performance or for those who depend on this software to exist, carrying out a stress test might be the difference between a positive and a negative experience for the user and determining its success, image, and reputation.

Spike Testing (Seasonal Peaks)

Spike testing is also one of the types of performance tests that can be carried out on a system. When this test is done, it will focus on the ability the software has to handle sudden and sharp increases in load or traffic. As the name suggests, unlike other types of performance testing, such as load testing, stress testing, and endurance testing, in which the focus is on testing a system's performance under sustained loads or gradually increasing loads, the spike test will look at a peak of access, such as in a promotion.

Remember when I used the example of the famous singer selling tickets to their shows? Well, this is an example of a spike test that was not performed. While the traffic on the website might be "normal" for some performers, if you are talking about, for example, a beloved band that hasn't played together in years or a performer that hasn't had presentations in a long time, this could lead to an increased demand for tickets—generating a spike.

A similar situation happens during "Black Friday" and "Cyber Monday," which are promotional campaigns to sell products at lower prices. Although this is not a situation that occurs normally, during these two events there might be a peak in access to a web page, for example, leading to a crash. Some companies, already aware of the increasing demand for online shopping from customers worldwide, usually prepare their systems for these events. This helps them avoid having the clients face problems such as downtime in the system and page crashes.

At the same time that this test will provide a good overview of the weaknesses of the system, you must also consider that it is designed for a specific reason, making it somewhat limited. Because of these limitations, the testing will not be as costly as other performance tests, but it can also be difficult to replicate because it is nearly impossible to predict user behavior —although some might try by using historic metrics. Finally, if the environment and the test are not carried out correctly, these might lead to mistakes in reading the results, generating more problems and inaccuracies in the outcome of the test.

Endurance Testing (Soak Testing)

When people say they are going to "soak in the bathtub," this usually means that they are going to stay there for some time. Well, when you consider **endurance testing**, or **soak testing**, you should think about a similar concept. This means that software will be tested by leaving it for a certain period of time—generally extended—under a determined load to see how it will perform. This test needs to be carried out specifically for software that will be used continuously, and, therefore, there is a need to see what its behavior will be when this happens.

One of the things that can happen with software over time is that it degrades or that it starts using too many resources, such as CPU processing. This can lead to a slower response time and more errors, including a complete system failure. For this reason, to ensure that the program is reliable over a certain period of time and that it will maintain its stability, it is essential to carry out this test before its deployment.

Unlike the stress test or the spike test, this test will not target a specific punctual increase in traffic but rather a continuous workload. Think about a company that is based in several countries and uses one integrated system for all of its employee databases. If all of them are constantly using the data that is contained there, can you imagine what would happen? If your guess is that the server could become overloaded and the system could start to fail, you are correct. Therefore, it will be essential to carry out the test with the longest stress period possible to identify its response.

For software that is used for outside clients, there must also be the assurance that it will be capable of handling a large, constant demand for a better customer experience. Imagine a new website, for example. How many people, do you think, access it to read the latest news at least once a day? If you add to this the fact that people from outside its host country might also access it, the possibilities are numerous. Therefore, it will be essential that it be prepared for this traffic to ensure that the pages do not crash.

One of the negative aspects of endurance testing is that it takes some time, considering its characteristics. This means that it might be left behind if there is a problem with the deadline to deliver the software. In addition to this, the system can become corrupted if there is an error, leading to problems in its structure and data loss, something that could incur costs for the company.

Finally, consider that it is almost impossible to mirror user behavior as it would happen in real life, and, therefore, this would be more of an estimate than an accurate evaluation.

Volume Testing (Flood Test)

While we have already seen the tests that can be performed when there are too many requests and users for a program, we should also think of these systems for one other thing: data. Therefore, it is essential that the volume of data that a system can handle be evaluated by the company before deployment. This type of test is called **volume testing** or **flood testing**. When this test is carried out, it will show the tester what the system's capacity to handle information is and up to what point it is stable, reliable, and performing efficiently.

Let's suppose that the client is a company that works with data science, which means they handle hundreds, if not thousands, of databases to manage the information for their projects. This means that the software needs to be capable of handling and processing all this data to ensure that they can carry out the analysis accurately and properly, without suffering database overload. In addition to this, the system should be able to handle the storage of this information without failing or losing it.

To think about a system that would benefit from this testing scenario, think about your country's most popular bank. Now imagine all the types of data it must deal with, from account holder details to the information pertaining to every single product each of these users has for all the accounts it has. When you think of it this way, it might be possible to understand why it is so important for this test to take place.

One of the capabilities that will be tested in the volume test is the scalability of the program and how it reacts with different volumes of data and what the system's response in each of these situations will be. Another item that will be tested is load balancing, or the capability that it has to distribute the workload among the company's different services to ensure that one is not overloaded. Of course we shouldn't forget about the performance after all; this is what will be mainly impacted if the program is flooded with information.

However, this test does not come without its disadvantages, and one of them is crucial to many companies: cost. This test can be costly because of its complexity, including the need of an extensive structure to carry it out—from personnel to equipment. Another thing that will be highly impacted is the efficiency of the test, since it can take a long time to execute and not necessarily all scenarios that will happen in real-life can be predicted to be tested. However, if a company expects software to handle large amounts of data, this test should certainly be part of the development strategy to ensure that the chances of a system failure are reduced to a minimum.

SECURITY TESTING

Even though the name of this test can be self-explanatory, there are some things that some people who are not testers do not even imagine are carried out when it is performed. **Security testing**, as the name suggests, must be carried out to ensure that the software being developed is safe for the user and for the company. I could even say that even if no other tests are performed, performing this one is essential. More than essential, it is critical, and therefore, it must be a part of the company's strategy.

The main reason for this is that if the software is integrated with the company's data, contains user information, or both, it might be susceptible to security breaches and attacks from malicious parties. And if you consider the leak of this type of information, it might be the most damaging for the organization's reputation. Users who do not feel safe leaving their data in a certain system will not use it, or if they do, unaware that security has not been tested, the company might be liable for divulging private information.

In some countries, this protection is part of laws and regulatory measures, which can also characterize a compliance feature. Think about how many times you have seen in the news that this or that company had a security breach, or that your web browser said that your password might be compromised and should be changed. Therefore, we could say that the main objective of security testing is to identify the vulnerabilities and weaknesses in software that could be exploited by hackers to compromise the confidentiality, integrity, and availability of the system.

Although security testing is similar to the other types of tests when structure is taken into consideration, there is one major difference: The tester should establish threat models to mimic the threats that it might be susceptible to. While the test is established by humans, the remainder of the testing process can be carried out by automation tools, since this is how hackers attack systems most of the time—with "worms" or "viruses" they create to infect the system.

There is also a difference when you consider the parties responsible for the execution of these tests. While the tester is still the tester, they must count on the help of the developers to ensure that the safety measures are put in place, the client to inform them about the parameters that they must comply with, and the security analysts to analyze the behavior of the system and work on establishing a contingency plan if a problem is ever identified. By working together as a team, it will be possible to help reduce the risk of data breaches, financial loss, and reputational damage.

As we will see in the following sections, there are a few specific tests to determine security testing, such as code review, ethical hacking, vulnerability and security scanning, penetration testing, fuzz testing, and many others. It will depend on the evaluation of the development team, together with the tester and the security analysts, to determine which of these tests should be carried out and the best approach to doing so.

Security Scanning

One of the first things that can be done regarding the safety of your system is to evaluate if there are any potential vulnerabilities by carrying out a **security scan**. When the tester carries out this scan, they will be able to verify if there are any "weak" spots in the system before they can be breached by malicious individuals. These security scans can include tests such as vulnerability scanning and penetration testing, both of which we will see more about now.

Vulnerability Scanning

Once a system is ready, it is essential to run a **vulnerability scan** to determine if there are any weaknesses that can be exploited. This means you can scan the network, the application, the system, or any application that you think might be vulnerable. When this is done, you significantly reduce the chances of exposing the company to attacks made by hackers.

For this scan, testers usually use an automated tool that will scan and analyze the information and test the different possible entries into the assets. You must think of it as scanning a physical facility for potential entrances by burglars or other ill-intentioned individuals. When this is carried out, all the doors, windows, and other openings that the home might have will be evaluated to make sure that they are safe for those who are living there. With software, the process is the same, but it is done electronically, where the possibility of unauthorized entrances is evaluated and prevented.

One of the main features of vulnerability scanning is that it must be constant, just as a virus scan is constantly running on your computer. The main reason for this is that there can be changes to the system that leave unattended possibilities. Once these openings are identified, they should be reported and scaled by the security team to establish their priority levels.

Based on each vulnerability priority—high, medium, or low—an action plan is established to correct them according to their importance. This should involve the developers, testers, security team, and client, who will help establish what is more important in the process. By doing this continuously throughout the SDLC, the company also saves money since they are taking proactive steps to prevent the risk of potential attacks. Therefore, taking action before the problem occurs will be an effective way to ensure that the risks are significantly minimized.

Penetration Testing

Another way to perform a security test is to carry out a simulated attack on certain of the system's areas, known as **penetration testing**. As the name might suggest, in this test, the security professional will try to access, or penetrate, the system through the vulnerable areas that are identified. This is a step that can be taken after the vulnerability scan to effectively measure the chances and possibilities of an attack. In addition to this, penetration testing will help provide validation for what was identified in the scan and ensure that the protective measures taken by the company are effective.

Therefore, when you think about this test, it should be a way of ensuring that the company is compliant with safety regulations and that the risks are correctly prioritized. The level of access that the testers will have will depend on the needs presented by the client—they can have more or less access, varying from testing the possibility of email servers to server infiltration. Because of the extensive reach this test can have, it is essential that the parameters be established before the testing takes place, where the client will tell the tester the specifications that should be looked at. This will make the process faster and ensure that there are no delays in delivering the feedback if quick action is needed.

When a penetration test is carried out, it will be thoroughly planned by a team that will try to gain access as a hacker would. They will first try to recognize and identify the system, and once this has been done, a scan will be run to evaluate the system's vulnerable areas. Next, the tester will try to gain and maintain access to the program. While entering is already a problem, it might not be as significant as keeping the intruder logged in since they will have better chances of gaining access to sensitive data. Because of this, the main idea is to remain connected for the longest period possible. Finally, once the test is finalized, the results will be analyzed and reported to the client, establishing where the problems were identified.

As I mentioned earlier, since this is an extensive test that requires time, it is also an expensive one since it demands that the professional who is carrying it out has the knowledge and the tools to do so. This means that they have undergone specific training and specialization to know the correct way to do this. Furthermore, since it is carried by an individual and not by a machine that takes a snapshot of the moment and not of the complete picture, it might give the organization the sense they are protected (or not), leading them to ignore other potential issues that may arise that were not looked into.

Security Audit/Review

A **security audit** or **review** has a similar process to a normal audit, but it targets the security of a system or software program. Similar to a security scan, this process has the main objective of identifying potential vulnerabilities in the company's assets and ensuring that the measures taken are compliant with the regulations and laws required by the location in which it is hosted. This assessment will usually be carried out by a team of security experts who will analyze if there are security measures in place and what are the contention actions that will be taken if a vulnerability is found or exploited by a malicious organization.

The audit is a planned process that will analyze documentation such as procedures and policies regarding safety. The auditor will ask questions that they see as relevant to the company's infrastructure and compare the answers to what they see in practice. Once they have reached a conclusion, they will create a risk assessment document that will identify if there are any risks, what their critical level is, and what actions should be taken to prevent any problems.

The company, once it receives this document, will need to carry out the suggested measures or alternatives it might identify to solve the issues. After the solutions have been implemented, a follow-up audit is usually carried out to see what steps have been taken to minimize the risks. If everything is compliant, the company might receive accreditation (if that is the case) or be considered to have "passed" the audit.

To carry out this audit, a company can proceed by creating a team that will analyze these internally and ask for external validation from a third party. In some companies, this process may be carried out inter-departmentally or by different locations evaluating each other's compliance and actions. In either the case of an external party or an in-company process, the reporting usually scales up to higher management, who will be responsible for evaluating the results and establishing an action plan and group to carry out the needed corrections.

Finally, the audit should be considered an important part of the security evaluation process since it is a documented procedure that ensures that the company is taking the necessary measures to avoid data loss and infiltration. In some countries, this audit is required by law, and organizations must abide by them. In others, it might not be legally required but will help enhance the company's reputation and give the users extra assurance that their data is protected.

Ethical Hacking

It is hard to imagine that there is something known as **ethical hacking**. This is because when we think about the term "hacking," we have all sorts of negative thoughts, generally envisioning things similar to what we see on television shows and movies. But rest assured that there are professionals in the market dedicated to this craft, also known as **white hat hacking**. These individuals will operate the same way that a malicious hacker would, except they are doing this to evaluate the programs' vulnerabilities and what can be improved in the system.

Although most users will not identify that this hack is happening, there are tools they use that you might recognize. Have you ever received a suspicious email in your inbox and did not click on it? If your company has the appropriate training, you probably didn't, and a few weeks later you received the following message, "Congratulations! You have passed our security test because you did not click on the link attached to the email sent on [place here the date]." This means that this was a targeted test, probably carried out by a hacker or the IT team, to see what percentage of users in the company **did** click and who needs to undergo more training.

By doing this, the hacker probably wanted to inject a virus that came with the link, which would in turn "invade" the system if the user clicked on it. By having users click on it, the hacker would have gained access to the company's system, just as a malicious individual would. Therefore, by doing this, they have exploited one vulnerable aspect, and the solution is to provide more personnel training.

With the increase in the number of hacks into large organizations' systems, ethical hacking has become essential if a company wants to accurately identify the vulnerabilities and possibilities of exposure. If you have seen the news about companies that have been exposed to ransomware or malware that released private data, you will certainly understand what I mean. This problem seems to become more frequent and common as time goes by, and it is likely because of a lack of efficient security measures or user mistakes.

An ethical hacker, just like a malicious one, has several tools under their belt to ensure that they can gain access to the company. What they do is use the items from their toolkit, such as gathering private user information, identifying vulnerabilities, exploring defective code, and hacking the server or the corporate wifi, to gain access to what they want. However, to do this and to ensure they are working for the "good guys," they need to have specific certifications, such as the Certified Ethical Hacker (CEH) certificate, or they can be a Certified Information Systems Security Professional (CISSP), all provided by accredited organizations that control their activities.

In addition to this, to be a software hacker, the professional must first and foremost be **ethical**. This means that they will not use the obtained information in a malicious manner or in a way that can negatively impact their clients. Apart from this, they must also be creative and persistent to find different ways to attack a system in a way that the company had not previously predicted. You must also add that they should have strong analytical and technical skills, since analyzing a system, or at least a part of it, might be different in every situation. This means they must be able to look at the software they are testing and see the potential breaches and what they can do to access it.

But ethical hacking is not perfect—it has some limitations, and these need to be considered as well when you think about carrying out this type of test. First and foremost, this is a process that is carried out by a human, which means that there might be flaws, especially because white hat hacking usually targets a specific part of the program, making it possible to overlook certain aspects of the software. This also means that the tests take some time, which might not be a good alternative if you are in a hurry—this could lead to certain issues being missed because a deadline had to be met.

API Security Testing

An application programming interface, or API, is one of the most important parts of software development since it is frequently used as a "connector" to communicate programs with each other. This means the code will be simplified without the need for extra lines by establishing specific definitions and protocols. Therefore, because of its characteristics, it will be essential to determine that they are safe and that there are no vulnerabilities, since it can also be considered a "back door" for malicious intruders.

Some of the things that should be looked at are how the API is performing when requests are made, what routes it is using to carry out communication, and how accurate the information it's conveying is. These tools can be either manual or hybrid, since some tests are unable to be performed just electronically. According to *What Is API Security Testing?* (n.d.), API testing should follow these parameters:

- Incorrect inputs, including in size, should not be accepted.
- Empty inputs should not be accepted.
- Only inputs within a certain range should be accepted.
- The expected output must be presented for the determined inputs.

In **API security testing**, some of the security tests I have already mentioned can also be applied, such as vulnerability scans and penetration testing. Other tests can include the evaluation of the mechanisms used to access the API and how it handles different data inputs.

Still, when considering data, there is a specific test called **fuzz testing** that involves loading the API with large amounts of data to see how it reacts when there is an input of random data into the system. Apart from these, it is always essential that the security configurations of the API are validated, thus the need to carry out a security scan.

Mobile Application Security

When was the last time you left home without your phone? Better yet, when was the last time that you checked your phone to see if your data was protected? While most of us rarely leave our homes without our mobile devices, I could also say that the number of people who validate that their phone is safe from hackers is minimal. This means that to ensure that your data is protected, it will be essential that mobile applications are safe and that they are not vulnerable to attacks or unauthorized access. To make sure that the risks are minimal, organizations should carry out **mobile application security** tests.

Many companies today, identifying that some people use their phones as their primary communication tool, are working to guarantee that their applications are not susceptible to data breaches or malware to protect the user data. Can you imagine the repercus-

198 | JAIME MANTILLA, MSIT

sions if your phone was breached because of an application vulnerability? This could severely damage a company's reputation, making thousands of users, if not more, uninstall it and leave bad ratings. This is an area that is constantly growing and demanding more testers in the market for both the development phase and to carry out subsequent tests after it has been deployed.

Some of the major aspects which are looked at during this test is how the user logs in and if this is efficient and safe, if the code is secure or if it provides breaches to malicious attackers, and if the data used is encrypted according to market standards. If you think about the amount of personal data you have on your phone, this is critical. We have access to bank applications, addresses, phone numbers, and pictures, to name a few.

Network Security Testing

The last type of test that I want to talk to you about is **network security testing**. When this test is performed, it aims at ensuring that the computer network is safe from threats and malicious activity. This means installing firewalls, encryption, and other security measures that will help ensure that if one computer is contaminated, the other in the network will be safe. This means that the tester must understand network architecture, security protocols, and tools used to manage and monitor network security.

Let's go back to the example of the user within a company that clicks on a malicious link they found in an email. If network protocols and security are not established, the hacker will be able to access other computers and even the server because of this simple mistake that the user made. Now, while all attacks are dangerous, imagine the damage that could be done if the hacker is able to control the computer network of a hospital! Imagine if they disabled access to the systems and the doctors were unable to access patient information for medication and treatment!

What if you escalate this possibility to other institutions such as banks, technology companies, governments, and energy providers? The impact that this can have on our lives and the reputations of the affected businesses is unimaginable. Furthermore, there is also the risk of losing intellectual property, sensitive information, user details, and all other types of data that may or may not be critical. Therefore, you must consider network testing as one of the items that must be included in the company's software development strategy.

By establishing and testing controls such as firewalls, VPNs, encryption, and access control, for example, the company is able to have a better idea of what is vulnerable and what is protected. This will make it easier to access weaknesses and also avoid any disruptions that might occur. Finally, it is also important to always remember to install antivirus and antimalware software that will help identify malicious attempts on the network, such as phishing and DDoS attacks.

8

BECOMING A SOFTWARE TESTER

Now that you have learned a lot about software testing, you may raise the question: *Would I be a good candidate for a position in this industry?* Well, the first thing is that you must **study**. A tester usually has knowledge about several areas and not only one specific type of test. This means that they are constantly polishing up their technical skills with learning programs and keeping up-to-date with the latest developments in the industry to ensure that the best service is provided.

However, as you will see, there are several other attributes that are necessary to ensure that you succeed in the area. This chapter will give you some clues to understand if you are a good fit and will also provide you with some tips on how to get a job in software testing. As a bonus, I have included a few common questions to help you prepare for potential job interviews, all of which you will find the answers to in this book. Are you ready to find out if there is a "match" between you and the testing profession? Let's check it out!

WOULD YOU BE A SUITABLE CANDIDATE TO BECOME A SOFTWARE TESTER?

After everything that you have read so far, if you want to pursue a career in software testing, you must be thinking about some of the soft skills that are required to pursue the profession. *What skills must I develop or have to become a tester?* This is a good question. The first thing you must know is that testing is more than studying and memorizing information—you will need to have analytical and critical thinking skills. On the other hand, these are skills you can learn since being a tester is not something you are naturally "born" with (Norrish, 2021).

Therefore, this is good news but also bad. It means that if you are set on starting in this profession, you will need to learn how to "think" like a tester. Yes, that is something. As Norrish (2021) says, testing "is an activity that some people seem to be better at than others—some people just seem to have a 'tester mentality'... they 'think like a tester.'" On the other hand, it is bad news because no amount of theoretical information will be useful if you don't have the ability to put it into practice. This is why having these qualities will be essential to success in your career.

To name a few of the characteristics that we will see, I could cite Knott (n.d.), who says that testers "have solid communication skills to adapt their language depending on the people they are talking to. Good software testers ask questions before and during the development phase to bring up unclear or implicit specifications." Let's take a deeper look into 10 of the most demanded soft skills and qualities that a tester should have to be successful in their career.

Qualities of a Good Tester

1. **Creative:** Some people say that you cannot be a good tester if you are not creative. If you think about all the possibilities that exist for a user to navigate a software, this means that many times you will need to "think outside the box" and put different hats on to test a system. You should not be a person who "sticks" to common procedures but rather finds alternative ways to see the different ways that a system can be used.

2. **Analytical mindset:** Having an analytical mindset might help ensure the success of the

testing phase. You must be able to look at the components of the system and understand its logic and the steps that can be taken to make it work. This means analyzing the issues you find and the reasons why this is so. When you have the ability to analyze a situation, it will also be easier to explain to others what happened and why certain errors are occurring. In addition to this, when you add logic to this mindset, you will be setting yourself up for success.

3. **Critical thinking:** Critical thinking means that you will challenge the primary assumptions that have been made and the logic process that should be followed. You must have all the information available to ensure that you understand what is needed and evaluate the issues that you identify correctly. This could mean that you need to tap into your intuition and see if what you are thinking is correct or not. Sometimes, this will also mean that you must change from a linear point of view to "color outside the lines" and see different ways to approach a problem and find solutions to it.

4. **Curious:** If you are not a curious person, it is likely that you will not be attracted to a career in software testing. A tester must be curious to understand why things work the way they do

and why the software works the way it does. This will help them understand the developer's reasoning as well as the client's requirements. When a software tester wants to know the "why" of things, this will make them a better professional because they will constantly be looking for ways to improve the quality of the software being developed or find bugs that could be overlooked. Because of this, it is always important that they ask questions, which is our next item.

5. **Asks questions:** Asking questions is one of the main characteristics of a good tester. When this professional starts asking questions to understand how a system works or the reasons for a certain decision, this can lead to improvements in the development process to ensure that the client is happy. In addition to this, involving the tester in the software development strategy from the beginning and putting them in touch with the client to understand the requirements will enable them to ask as many questions as necessary to ensure that the main requirements are met and that the client is satisfied with the final result.

6. **Focused on the customer:** I have already mentioned the client a few times, and you must

understand why this is important. The client is the person who is paying for your services and can bring more opportunities if they are happy with the final result. Therefore, it is essential that the tester always keep in mind what the customer wants and what their needs are. Placing the client in first place when you consider software that is being tested will help ensure that the final result is satisfactory, increasing the company's reputation—both yours and theirs. Therefore, having a mindset that is focused on guaranteeing their satisfaction is essential.

7. **Pays attention to detail:** Having a mind that is trained to look at details will be essential for a tester. This is because when you are testing software, you must check that the minimal things are free from potential bugs. It is from this attention to detail that the quality of the software and, consequently, client satisfaction will be determined.

8. **Flexible:** Testing is not always a straightforward process. This means that you must be able to find bugs where they were not imagined and be flexible enough to explore other opportunities that might present themselves during the testing phase. This

means that you could be carrying out one test and identify that there is a related issue that was not identified but still exists. When this happens, you must "free yourself" from the attached strings of following the plan as strictly determined and see what the problem is, even if it was not part of the scope. You must remember that your motivation should come from ensuring that the final product has quality and that the customer is satisfied with the final result.

9. **Team player:** A software tester does not work on their own. They must know how to collaborate with the development team, the project manager, the client, and several other stakeholders involved in the process. If they do not know how to work as a team, it is likely that the chances of success will be reduced, since this skill is essential to guaranteeing that the processes are performed in due time and that there are no delays. Furthermore, it is not only essential to know how to work as a team but also to know how to communicate with them, as we will see in the next item.

10. **Communicative:** Being able to communicate what you have identified in a simple and direct way will be one of the major skills that you can

have as a tester. Sometimes, the developer does not want to know all the minor details of how the bug was found but prefers to have an overview of what the problem is and why it happened. The software development industry is working fast with constant innovation, and there is no time to lose. Therefore, when you enhance your communication skills, you must be able to do so in an efficient and polite manner, since the information you have to share is not always what developers want to hear. Work on your verbal and written communication, being aware that others must understand what you mean without further explanation, and what the process was that led to a particular problem.

HOW TO GET A JOB IN SOFTWARE TESTING

As I mentioned when you started reading, there is not really a specific test or graduate course that you can take to become a software tester. This will very much depend on your career path, your abilities, and, of course, what you have studied. In the market, there are professional testers with the most varied backgrounds, from computer science to engineering and business. It will all depend on the type of software testing that you want to carry out or specialize in. According to a study carried out by Florea & Stray (2019), who studied the market for testing jobs, "the overwhelming majority of employers asked for testing-related competence from testers, followed closely by technical skills. Two thirds of the ads asked for soft skills, and only one third of the ads sought domain-specific skills."

Suppose that you want to deal with security. This means that apart from being educated in a relevant field, you will also need to undergo specific training sessions related to security in testing and maybe even get certified. On the other hand, if you are talking about testing for usability, a course in user experience (UX) might be the way to go since it will cover some of the main aspects users look for when using a specific piece of software. You could also have a degree in design, for example, as it would help you see the best way to approach a platform's visual configuration and access.

Although I have already told you that you don't necessarily need to know how to code for testing, it might be a great advantage to know how to. As you have seen, some testing techniques require code to be analyzed and evaluated, and knowing how to do so can help you. For this reason, there are many testers who come from a computer science background, because they know the basics of how a system operates and can build on this knowledge. Most of the time, testers are required to have a programming or engineering background (69.0%) or knowledge of programming languages or technologies (42.2%) (Florea & Stray, 2019).

If you don't come from any of these backgrounds, you could get into the area by attending testing-oriented bootcamps that will give you the essential tools to understand how to enter the profession. They will teach you some of the basics, and you will have to continue learning and educating yourself in order to grow in your career. This might be a good alternative for people who do not have the time to undergo other forms of formal education. While these will provide a broad spectrum of testing areas, they also pose an advantage because they will be focused exclusively on testing. Therefore, using this route might get all the information you need to start your career.

It is important to have knowledge about the testing process, test management, test types, and tools, and this might be important to ensure that you have success in obtaining a job. Still, according to Florea & Stray (2019), the following skills were requested by job posters when considering the knowledge obtained by software testers: 87.2% were expected to have knowledge about the testing process, 72.2% should have test management skills, 65.7% were required to know about testing types, and 59.5% said they asked for skills related to test tools.

In addition to this, you might want to consider getting certified as a tester, such as the Certified Manager of Software Testing (CMST), International Software Testing Qualifications Board (ISTQB) Tester, Certified Software Tester (CSTE), or even the white hat ethical certification (Indeed, 2022). To start off, might I suggest that you look up the ISTQB Foundation Level (CTFL) course that will give you the basic information on software testing that requires no specific skills and is open to anyone?

Next, you might want to consider the relevant work experience you have and the skills you have gained throughout your professional life. As I told you, the path of the software tester usually begins as a QA assurance professional that rises in the ranks as they gain experience and moves from general QA to more specific testing tasks. If you are still unsure, you might want to connect with some software testers in the market whom you know and learn more about the market. Much like in any profession, networking is essential.

Finally, if you still lack experience and are looking for some practice, you will find that several companies offer "challenges" to non-employees that consist of trying to find vulnerabilities in their systems. While this might not be a "real" testing experience, you might be able to start getting an idea of how the profession works. Some companies that work with cyber security work with ethical hacking programs and challenges that their clients hire them to perform. If you are starting, this might be one way to go and give you at least some market experience to demonstrate in your new CV.

COMMON INTERVIEW QUESTIONS AND ANSWERS

To finalize this chapter and before we move on to the conclusion of the book, I would like to share with you 15 of the most common questions that are asked in interview processes if you are applying to be a software tester. All of the answers to these questions can be found in this book. Ready? Read on!

1. What are the two different types of software testing? Can you name two examples of each?

Answer: The two types of software testing are functional and non-functional. Two examples of functional testing include API testing and integration testing, and two types of non-functional testing include maintainability and compatibility testing. *For more examples, refer to Chapters 6 and 7, which talk about functional and non-functional testing.*

2. What is the relationship between a unit test, a component test, and a system test, and when would you carry each one out?

Answer: All of these tests are considered functional tests that will be applied to different parts of the system. The unit test will examine a small piece of the code, the component test will look at a larger part of the code, and the system test consists of testing the full system and its functionalities. Each of these tests should be performed throughout the software development process to ensure that when you carry out the next one, there are the fewest bugs possible. *For a deeper understanding, refer to Chapter 6 of this book.*

3. Within the software testing process, what are some of the steps that should not be missed in the test plan?

Answer: In the software testing process, the tester should follow six steps that are essential to ensuring the correct development of the procedure. They are requirement analysis, test planning, test case development, test environment setup, test execution, and test closure. *To learn more about what each of these steps entails, refer to Chapter 2, under the What is the Software Testing Life Cycle section.*

4. Can you tell me the difference between white box, black box, and grey box testing? In which cases would they best be applied?

Answer: Black box testing means that you will test the software without looking specifically into the coding details of the program. On the other hand, when you carry out white box testing, you will look at the code and its details to ensure there are no problems. Finally, for grey box testing, it will be a hybrid of te black box and white box testing that will look at parts of the code as well as the inputs and outputs of the system. *I approach these three types of tests in Chapter 6, under the Other Functionality Tests section.*

5. Is it possible to have a system that is 100% bug free? If so, how would you do it?

Answer: No, it is not possible to have a system that is 100% bug free. The tester can do their best to ensure that there are the fewest errors possible, but it is virtually impossible to ascertain that a system is 100% bug free. *More information on this throughout the book, but specifically under Myth #3 in Chapter 4.*

6. For which type of test would you carry out an automated or a manual procedure? Explain the rationale behind your decision.

Answer: The decision between carrying out an automated or manual test will depend on the time that the tester has to carry out the process and the type of test that they will run, as well as the system's stability. Automated testing is better suited for systems that are stable. If the system is being worked on, there is a possibility that the automated test will break frequently. For example, in an ethical hack test, the testing will generally be manual, while in a security scan, it is possible to have the test 100% automated. In addition to this, the budget that the company has will determine how much labor time can be dedicated to testing. Finally, the tester may be able to automate some repetitive tests. *More information on manual and automation testing can be found in Chapter 5, Common Types of Software Testing.*

7. Can you describe what regression testing is and when you would apply it?

Answer: Regression testing is the process of checking that what was previously done is not impacted by the new features that were created for the program. This means checking that the new code does not negatively impact or create a bug for something that already existed and was tested. It should be carried out throughout the development process to ensure that the new features do not impact the parts of the software that were already developed. *For more information on regression testing, refer to the section Regression Testing in Chapter 6.*

8. What is load testing, and how does it differ from a spike test?

Answer: Load testing is one type of performance testing that focuses specifically on how the system will respond when too much information is being processed and how much the system can support regarding the different types of loads. On the other hand, a spike test will test the system when there is a peak in requests for the system, and it will test how much load the system can support in a specific context, such as promotions or campaigns. *More information on* *the differences can be found in Chapter 6, under the Performance Testing section.*

9. Suppose your company is about to deploy software. What would be the last test you would recommend be carried out, and why?

Answer: (This will be based on your opinion as a tester, but here I will present two valid answers.)

A. I would carry out an end-to-end test to ensure that the full system works from start to finish and that the inputs generate the correct outputs. *For more information on end-to-end testing, please refer to Chapter 6.*

B. I would carry out a usability test with the user to ensure that the system meets the requirements and that everything is according to the specifications that were provided. I consider this to be the last test because this is when the client will give their final feedback. *To obtain more information about usability tests, refer to Chapter 7.*

10. What is an API, and why should it be tested?

Answer: An API is an application programming interface that serves as a connector between different components of software and is used in modern system design. This test should be carried out to ensure that there are no communication issues between the different parts of the program, that the information flows without any problems, and where the input generates the expected output. *Please refer to Chapter 6, under the API Testing section, for more information on this test.*

11. What is security testing, and why should it be carried out? Can you name two different security tests and their advantages?

Answer: Security testing is the process that is carried out to ensure that the software being developed is safe for the user and for the company from malicious intruders and potential attacks. Two different types of security tests are vulnerability scans, where the tester will run a scan in the program to determine what the vulnerabilities of the system are and potential entrances that are more likely to be threatened, and penetration testing, where the security professional will try to access, or penetrate, the system through the vulnerable areas that are identified. *More information on security testing and its different types can be found in Chapter 7, Non-Functional Testing.*

12. If you are carrying out a test and you find a bug, what should you do?

Answer: The first thing you should do is try to replicate it. If it is possible, then you must write a bug report that establishes the process that led to the bug and a detailed description of the error that is identified. Ensure that this is a bug in the system, categorize it, and communicate it to the development department so that they can proceed with fixing the error. *To find more information on Chapter 3 under Software Quality Defect Management Approach.*

13. What is the difference between software testing and quality assurance?

Answer: Software testing and SQA are both important aspects of product development, although they serve different purposes. Software testing is the process of identifying defects or bugs in software by running tests on it. In this case, the main objective will be to identify and fix defects before the software is released to users. SQA is the process of ensuring that software products meet their specified requirements and are as free as possible from defects. It involves the development of processes, procedures, and standards so that software presented to the final client is of high quality. *More information on software testing and SQA can be found in Chapter 3, under the section with the same name.*

14. Should testing be carried out only when the software is ready? Why or why not?

Answer: No. The testing process should never be left until the end of the development process. Software testing is essential to the software development strategy to ensure that the client receives a quality product that is as free from bugs as possible. Software testers should be involved in the process from the beginning to ensure that they are aware of client requirements and that they are met. *To understand more about this question, please refer to Chapter 4, Myth #4, which approaches this subject.*

15. When is testing not necessary as a part of the software development strategy?

Answer: Never. Software testing should always be considered part of the SDLC. It will be important to improve the software's quality, reduce costs, improve customer satisfaction, enhance business reputations, and ensure regulatory compliance for the program that is being developed. *For more information on the importance of the STLC, refer to Chapter 2 of this book.*

CONCLUSION

Congratulations on making it to the end of this book! You are now one step closer to becoming a software tester. With the information I have provided you in this book, you will be able to take the first steps toward enhancing or changing your career. Remember that it does not matter what your age is or where you are in your professional life; if you have the right skills, you are perfectly able to become a software tester. The first move you have already made—to learn more and become acquainted with the details of what a software tester does and some of the tests that can be carried out.

In this book, you have learned about the history of software testing and its importance to software development. I have talked about the SDLC and the STLC and each of the steps that make up these processes. It will be essential to remember that for software to be productive, you must integrate testing into the strategy from the beginning. This does not mean that the software will be completely bug-free, since we have already seen that such a thing does not exist. Talking about some other things that are complete myths in the software testing area, you have read a whole chapter about some of the common things that people believe about software testing that are not true.

In addition to this, the next half of the book was composed of all of the different types of software testing and what each of them entails. You have read about game testing, mobile testing, AI testing, and so much more! You mustn't forget that we also approached the two types of testing that software can undergo: functional and non-functional testing. In each of these dedicated chapters, you have seen comprehensive information on the types of tests that belong to each category and their importance to the process.

Even though we covered a lot of testing strategies and techniques, in the real world not all of them are implemented based on project size and budget. There are testing techniques and strategies that are more common than others. However, being familiar with them is important so you can speak to specific organizations and educate stakeholders about them in case needed.

My suggestion for you is to identify which of these you can relate to more and start working! Learn more information and see if your skills match the needs that these require. Talking about skills, in the last chapter we looked at the main skills that companies look for in a tester. Remember: No one is born a tester! With practice and dedication, you can develop the necessary skills to thrive in this career and go beyond what you imagined. To give you some support, I have provided a final section with the most common questions and answers that are asked by newcomers in the industry.

Now, it is all up to you! If you are still looking for where to start and you have no experience in the area, I would suggest that you look for online courses and bootcamps you can participate in to gain experience. Keep in mind that networking will be essential for your career to grow and to meet new professionals who can show you market details. If you have coding experience or an engineering or computer software background, you might want to look up some shorter courses and start practicing with some of the examples I have given you. It is all in your hands!

I can safely say that while it is a demanding path, it is also full of rewards. Look at my journey; I made it, and so can you! It is possible! All it takes is some dedication and practice, and I am sure that you will thrive. Maybe someday it will be me reading the book you wrote about your testing experience; who knows?

If you liked this book, I ask that you please leave a review so that others can be confident that the content you have read here will help them learn more about this industry. Apart from that, I wish you good luck and much success on your new journey!

REFERENCES

A comprehensive guide to disaster recovery testing. (2021, November 23). EnsureDR. https://www.ensuredr.com/a-comprehensive-guide-to-disaster-recovery-testing/

Abu Sayed Mahfuz. (2020). *Software Quality Assurance: Integrating Testing, Security, and Audit.* Auerbach.

Altvater, A. (2020). *What is SDLC? Understand the software development life cycle.* Stackify. https://stackify.com/what-is-sdlc/

An introduction to software testing life cycle (STLC): Definition and phases. (n.d.). Sealights. https://www.sealights.io/software-quality/an-introduction-to-software-testing-life-cycle-stlc-definition-and-phases/

Anand, B. (2023, March 6). *How to become a software tester? Skills, job profiles, duties.* Knowledge Hut. https://www.knowledgehut.com/blog/software-testing/how-to-become-software-tester

Banu, S. (2022, June 27). *A complete guide to software testing life cycle (STLC).* LambdaTest. https://www.lambdatest.com/blog/software-testing-life-cycle/

Bartlett, J. (2021, February 25). *Characteristics of a good software tester.* TestLodge. https://blog.testlodge.com/characteristics-good-software-tester/

Best practices for disaster recovery testing. (2022, September 23). Snyk. https://snyk.io/learn/disaster-recovery-testing-best-practices/

Big Bang Integration Testing. (2022, November 14). *History of software testing.* GeeksforGeeks. https://www.geeksforgeeks.org/history-of-software-testing/

Black box testing. (n.d.). Javatpoint. https://www.javatpoint.com/black-box-testing

Boog, J. (2019, September 5). *9 types of software testing in software engineering.* The QA Lead. https://theqalead.com/test-management/types-of-software-testing/

Bose, S. (2022, September 30). *How to perform localization testing.* BrowserStack. https://www.browserstack.com/guide/localization-testing-on-websites-and-apps

Brewster, C. (n.d.). *Software quality assurance: What is it and why is it important?* Trio Developers. https://www.trio.dev/blog/software-quality-assurance

Bultman, A. (2022, June 23). *Learn about the concepts of testing gaming apps.* Headspin. https://www.headspin.io/blog/game-testing-a-complete-guide-to-its-types-and-processes

Bureau of Labor Statistics. (2018, April 13). *Software developers: Occupational outlook handbook.* Bls.gov; U.S. Bureau of Labor Statistics. https://www.bls.gov/ooh/computer-and-information-technology/software-developers.htm

Chawla, R. (2021, October 13). *Key performance testing Metrics: Why it matters and how to use them.* QAonCloud. https://www.qaoncloud.com/performance-testing-metrics/

Codoid. (2019, August 14). *The basics of software quality attributes.* Codoid. https://codoid.com/software-testing/the-basics-of-software-quality-attributes/

Comparison-STLC and SDLC. (n.d.). Tutorialspoint. https://www.tutorialspoint.com/stlc/stlc_sdlc_comparison.htm

Compatibility testing. (n.d.). Javatpoint. https://www.javatpoint.com/compatibility-testing

Compatibility testing guide | Tools, types & examples. (2022, May 17). Diffy. https://diffy.website/blog/compatibility-testing

Cooper, M. W. (n.d.). *7 critical skills for QA testing career survival.* TechBeacon. https://techbeacon.com/app-dev-testing/7-soft-skills-every-qa-tester-needs

Crispin, L., & Gregory, J. (2009). *Agile testing: a practical guide for testers and agile teams.* Addison-Wesley.

Defect management process: How to manage a defect effectively. (2023, February 13). Software Testing Help. https://www.softwaretestinghelp.com/defect-management-process/

Defect management tutorial: A comprehensive guide with examples And Best

Practices. (n.d.). Lambda Test. https://www.lambdatest.com/learn ing-hub/defect-management

Difference between globalization testing and localization testing. (n.d.). Javatpoint. https://www.javatpoint.com/globalization-testing-vs-localization-testing

Dilmegani, C. (2023, January 4). *Complete guide on AI in software testing: Benefits & challenges.* AI Multiple. https://research.aimultiple.com/ai-testing/

Disaster recovery testing for managed service providers. (n.d.). MSP360 Blog. https://www.msp360.com/resources/blog/disaster-recovery-testing/

Divyanshu_gupta1. (2021, July 15). *Software development life cycle (SDLC).* GeeksforGeeks. https://www.geeksforgeeks.org/software-development-life-cycle-sdlc/

Dosaj, C. (2019). *A Self-Study Guide For The ISTQB Foundation Exam Certified Tester Foundation Level (CTFL) 2018 Syllabus.*

Doshi, K. (2023, March 22). *Types of software testing : Learn with examples.* BrowserStack. https://www.browserstack.com/guide/types-of-testing

8 essential skills to look for in a top QA engineer. (2022, February 22). TestGorilla. https://www.testgorilla.com/blog/qa-engineer-skills/

Erin. (2021, September 24). *What's AI testing? A web developer's guide to AI-powered testing.* Testim. https://www.testim.io/blog/whats-ai-testing/

Expert Panel. (2022, November 3). *Eight cybersecurity checkups your company should conduct regularly.* Forbes. https://www.forbes.com/sites/theyec/2022/11/03/eight-cybersecurity-checkups-your-company-should-conduct-regularly/?sh=2397f4aa57ce

Felice, S. (2022, October 17). *What is sanity testing with examples.* BrowserStack. https://www.browserstack.com/guide/sanity-testing

Florea, R., & Stray, V. (2019). The skills that employers look for in software testers. *Software Quality Journal.* https://doi.org/10.1007/s11219-019-09462-5

Game testing 101: Basic tips and strategies. (n.d.). Starloop Studios. https://starloopstudios.com/game-testing-101-tips-and-strategies/

Gayatri. (2023, March 10). *Software quality testing (SQT) - An overview*. Acme Study. http://www.acmestudy.com/2023/03/software-qual ity-testing-sqt-overview.html

GeeksforGeeks. (2017, August). *Types of software testing*. https://www. geeksforgeeks.org/types-software-testing/

Ghoshal, P. (2022, May 31). *5 reasons why you should become a software tester*. FDM Group. https://www.fdmgroup.com/blog/5-reasons-why-you-should-become-a-software-tester/

González, J. P. (2022, June 9). *How to prioritize performance with failover testing*. Foreworth. https://blog.foreworth.com/how-to-prioritize-performance-with-failover-testing

Grey box testing. (n.d.-a). Javatpoint. https://www.javatpoint.com/grey-box-testing

Grey box testing. (n.d.-b). Tutotialspoint. https://www.tutorialspoint. com/software_testing_dictionary/grey_box_testing.htm

Hamilton, T. (2023a, February 11). *Defect management process in software testing (bug report template)*. Guru 99. https://www.guru99.com/ defect-management-process.html

Hamilton, T. (2023b, February 11). *How to create a test plan (with example)*. Guru 99. https://www.guru99.com/what-everybody-ought-to-know-about-test-planing.html

Hamilton, T. (2023c, March 4). *STLC - Software testing life cycle phases & entry, exit criteria*. Guru 99. https://www.guru99.com/software-test ing-life-cycle.html

Hamilton, T. (2023d, March 11). *Sanity testing vs smoke testing: Introduction and differences*. Guru 99. https://www.guru99.com/ smoke-sanity-testing.html

Hamilton, T. (2023e, March 11). *Types of software testing: 100 examples of different testing types*. Guru99. https://www.guru99.com/types-of-software-testing.html

Hernandez, D. A. (2020, November 25). *History of software testing*. Medium. https://davidmoremad.medium.com/history-of-soft ware-testing-cfa461c4ae0a

Honda, M. (2014, January 29). *Soft Skills for Testers*. KMS Technology. https://kms-technology.com/testing/soft-skills-for-testers.html

How much does a software tester make? (2022, September 15). Glassdoor. https://www.glassdoor.com/Salaries/software-tester-salary-SRCH_KO0,15.htm

Hutcheson, M. L. (2003). *Software Testing Fundamentals*. John Wiley & Sons.

IBM. (2019). *What is software testing?* https://www.ibm.com/topics/software-testing

Imperva. (n.d.). *Black box testing*. https://www.imperva.com/learn/application-security/black-box-testing/

Indeed. (2022, September 15). *How to become a software tester (With Essential Skills)*. https://ca.indeed.com/career-advice/finding-a-job/how-to-become-software-tester

International Organization for Standardization. (2017). *ISO/IEC 12207:2008*. ISO. https://www.iso.org/standard/43447.html

Isbilen, E. (2022, December 27). *What is software quality assurance?* BuiltIn. https://builtin.com/software-engineering-perspectives/software-quality-assurance

Javatpoint. (2011). *SDLC - Software development life cycle*. https://www.javatpoint.com/software-engineering-software-development-life-cycle

KanikaVatsyayan. (2020, April 20). *Top 8 soft skills that every software tester must have*. Simple Programmer. https://simpleprogrammer.com/soft-skills-software-tester/?utm_content=cmp-true

Kirianova, M. (2019, November 22). *9 soft skills every QA professional needs*. HackerNoon. https://hackernoon.com/9-soft-skills-every-qa-professional-needs-1q533xlm

Kirilenko, I. (2022, September 27). *Artificial intelligence in software testing & API automation*. Parasoft. https://www.parasoft.com/blog/what-is-artificial-intelligence-in-software-testing/

Knott, D. (n.d.). *What makes a good tester great?* PractiTest. https://www.practitest.com/blog/what-makes-a-good-tester-great/

Krüger, N. (2018, November 20). *What is non functional testing?* Perforce Software. https://www.perforce.com/blog/alm/what-non-func

tional-testing

Maintainability testing. (n.d.). TMap. https://www.tmap.net/building-blocks/maintainability-testing

Manual testing. (n.d.). Javatpoint. https://www.javatpoint.com/manual-testing

Martey, R. (2022, December 6). *10 qualities of a good security program*. Forbes. https://www.forbes.com/sites/forbestechcouncil/2022/12/06/10-qualities-of-a-good-security-program/?sh=1c19658a1139

Martin, M. (2020, January 16). *Software development life cycle (SDLC) phases & models*. Guru 99. https://www.guru99.com/software-development-life-cycle.html.

McPeak, A. (2017, June 22). *12 reasons to pursue a software testing career*. SmartBear. https://smartbear.com/blog/reasons-software-testing-career/

Medewar, S. (2022, December 12). *What is software testing? Definition, types, benefits, approaches*. Hackr.io. https://hackr.io/blog/what-is-software-testing

Meyer, A. (2023, January 25). *20 soft skills every QA professional should have*. Carrerist. https://www.careerist.com/insights/20-soft-skills-every-qa-professional-should-have

Meyer, K. (2022, October 3). *Types of software testing: Different testing Types with details*. American Technology Consulting. https://blog.american-technology.net/types-of-software-testing/

MKS075. (2022, December 26). *Software engineering | Software quality assurance*. GeeksforGeeks. https://www.geeksforgeeks.org/software-engineering-software-quality-assurance/

Mosconi, N. (2022, November). *The importance of software testing*. Devlane. https://www.devlane.com/blog/the-importance-of-software-testing

Myers, G. J., Sandler, C., & Badgett, T. (2012). *The Art of Software Testing*. John Wiley & Sons. http://www.51testing.com/N_download/lib/TestingTechDL/ArtofSoftwareTesting.pdf

Naeem, A. (2023). *What is maintainability testing?* Educative. https://www.educative.io/answers/what-is-maintainability-testing

Naik, K., & Tripathy, P. (2008). *Software Testing and Quality Assurance: Theory and Practice.* Wiley. https://www.softwaretestinggenius. com/download/staqtpsn.pdf

Nanda, V. (2021a, June 9). *What is interface testing (types & example)?* Tutorialspoint. https://www.tutorialspoint.com/what-is-interface-testing-types-and-example

Nanda, V. (2021b, November 20). *Defect management process in software testing.* TutorialsPoint. https://www.tutorialspoint.com/defect-management-process-in-software-testing

Narasimman, P. (2023, January 30). *Different types of software testing with examples.* Knowledge Hut. https://www.knowledgehut.com/blog/software-testing/types-of-software-testing

9 common software testing myths and facts. (2023, February 18). Software Testing Help. https://www.softwaretestinghelp.com/myths-about-being-software-tester/

Norrish, B. (2021, October 15). *How to think like a tester.* Medium. https://medium.com/@blakenorrish/how-to-think-like-a-tester-7a174ff6aeaf

Northeastern University Graduate Program. (2018, August 23). *Working in quality assurance: Skills you need to robot-proof your career.* https://www.northeastern.edu/graduate/blog/quality-assurance-skills/

Palamarchuk, S. (2016, January 28). *The ultimate list of 100 software testing quotes.* Abstracta Software Testing Services. https://abstracta. us/blog/tools/ultimate-list-100-software-testing-quotes/#Funny_Testing_Quotes

Pandey, S. (2022, October 3). *Why is maintainability in testing important? How to achieve it?* BrowserStack. https://www.browserstack.com/guide/maintainability-testing

Parthiban, P. (2021, April 14). *7 reasons why software testing is important.* Indium Software. https://www.indiumsoftware.com/blog/why-software-testing/

Performance testing metrics | A detailed guide for businesses. (2023, March 24). TestingXperts. https://www.testingxperts.com/blog/performance-testing-metrics

Pittet, S. (2019). *The different types of testing in Software*. Atlassian. https://www.atlassian.com/continuous-delivery/software-testing/types-of-software-testing

Pp_pankaj. (2019, May 8). *Software testing | Non-functional testing*. GeeksforGeeks. https://www.geeksforgeeks.org/software-testing-non-functional-testing/

Pp_pankaj. (2021, February 19). *Myths about Software Testing*. GeeksforGeeks. https://www.geeksforgeeks.org/myths-about-software-testing/

Pp_pankaj. (2022, June 1). *Difference between SDLC and STLC*. GeeksforGeeks. https://www.geeksforgeeks.org/difference-between-sdlc-and-stlc/

Pp_pankaj. (2023a, February 6). *Sanity testing | Software testing*. GeeksforGeeks. https://www.geeksforgeeks.org/sanity-testing-software-testing/

Pp_pankaj. (2023b, March 13). *Software testing life cycle (STLC)*. GeeksforGeeks. https://www.geeksforgeeks.org/software-testing-life-cycle-stlc/

QAble. (2021, September 8). *Software testing myths and facts!* https://www.qable.io/software-testing-myths-and-facts/

Quality quotient of a tester: 22 core strengths to be a good tester. (2023, March 22). Software Testing Help. https://www.softwaretestinghelp.com/quality-quotient-of-tester/

Rajkumar. (2023a, January 1). *Entry and exit criteria in the process of STLC*. Software Testing Material. https://www.softwaretestingmaterial.com/entry-and-exit-criteria/

Rajkumar. (2023b, January 1). *What are quality attributes in software architecture*. Software Testing Material. https://www.softwaretestingmaterial.com/quality-attributes-in-software-architecture/

Rajkumar. (2023c, January 1). *What is software testing life cycle (STLC)*. Software Testing Material. https://www.softwaretestingmaterial.com/stlc-software-testing-life-cycle/

Rana, K. (2023, March 22). *Types of testing | Top 100 software testing types*. ArtOfTesting. https://artoftesting.com/types-of-testing

RedLine13. (2017, October 17). *Load testing vs. scalability testing and*

other testing models. RedLine13. https://www.redline13.com/blog/
2017/10/load-testing-vs-scalability-testing-and-other-testing-
models/

Roman, A. (2018). *A Study Guide to the ISTQB® Foundation Level 2018
Syllabus : Test Techniques and Sample Mock Exams.* Springer
International Publishing.

Sargeant, A. (2021, June 17). *9 benefits of software testing and quality
assurance.* ETestware. https://www.etestware.com/benefits-of-soft
ware-testing/

Satyabrata_Jena. (2021, October 20). *Failover testing in software testing.*
GeeksforGeeks. https://www.geeksforgeeks.org/failover-testing-
in-software-testing/

Scalability testing. (n.d.). Javatpoint. https://www.javatpoint.com/scala
bility-testing

*Scalability testing tutorial: A comprehensive guide with examples And Best
Practices.* (n.d.). Lambda Test. https://www.lambdatest.com/learn
ing-hub/scalability-testing

Schmitt, J. (2022, April 20). *Functional vs non-functional software testing.*
CircleCI. https://circleci.com/blog/functional-vs-non-functional-
testing/?utm_source=google&utm_medium=sem&utm_campaign=
sem-google-dg--emea-en-dsa-tROAS-auth-nb&utm_term=g_-
_c__dsa_&utm_content=&gclid=
Cj0KCQjwocShBhCOARIsAFVYq0iWgeNCESb_60Ec7B2o
M09XZuhSppKWd_LhqhW5kj0fZEluhytd8wAaAnhVEALw_wcB

SDLC vs STLC. (n.d.). Javatpoint. https://www.javatpoint.com/sdlc-vs-
stlc

SDLC vs STLC-What's the Difference. (n.d.). Tutorials Point. https://
www.tutorialspoint.com/sdlc-vs-stlc-what-s-the-difference

SDLC vs STLC: What's the difference? (2022, September 1). InterviewBit.
https://www.interviewbit.com/blog/sdlc-vs-stlc/

Security testing. (n.d.). Javatpoint. https://www.javatpoint.com/security-
testing

Semah, B. (2019). *Types of software testing: Different testing types with
details.* Hackr.io. https://hackr.io/blog/types-of-software-testing

Severns, R. (2021, May 14). *API security testing overview and tooling guide.*

StackHawk. https://www.stackhawk.com/blog/api-security-testing-overview/

Shain, D. (2021, April 15). *What is mobile testing?* Applitools. https://applitools.com/blog/what-is-mobile-testing/

Sharma, J. (2022, July 5). *Difference between software testing and quality assurance.* Shiksha. https://www.shiksha.com/online-courses/articles/difference-between-software-testing-and-quality-assurance/

Sharma, L. (2019, September 3). *Why is testing necessary and important?* TOOLSQA. https://www.toolsqa.com/software-testing/istqb/why-is-testing-necessary/

Simonova, M. (2022, August 12). *The distinction between testing and quality assurance in the software industry.* Forbes. https://www.forbes.com/sites/forbestechcouncil/2022/08/12/the-distinction-between-testing-and-quality-assurance-in-the-software-industry/?sh=50fe279d391d

Simplilearn. (2023a, February 20). *What is software quality assurance: Definition, benefits, and top techniques explained.* https://www.simplilearn.com/software-quality-assurance-article

Simplilearn. (2023b, February 23). *Sanity testing vs. smoke testing: What is it & differences.* https://www.simplilearn.com/sanity-testing-vs-smoke-testing-article

Singhsonalmeenu. (2022, October 4). *Benefits of Software Testing.* GeeksforGeeks. https://www.geeksforgeeks.org/benefits-of-software-testing/

Software quality management - quick guide. (2019). Tutorialspoint. https://www.tutorialspoint.com/software_quality_management/software_quality_management_quick_guide.htm

Software testing - myths. (n.d.). Tutorialspoint. https://www.tutorialspoint.com/software_testing/software_testing_myths.htm

Software Testing Fundamentals. (2023, March 15). *Software Testing Myths.* https://softwaretestingfundamentals.com/software-testing-myths/

Software testing myths — Learn with examples. (n.d.). Tuskr. https://tuskr.app/learn/software-testing-myths

Srinivasan, N. (2023, March 13). *Compatibility testing: Definition, types &*

process. Hurix Digital. https://www.hurix.com/compatibility-test ing-definition-types-process/

Synopsys. (2019). *What is the software development life cycle (SDLC) and how does it work?* https://www.synopsys.com/glossary/what-is-sdlc.html

Syvynska, N. (2022, June 28). *Top 10 popular software testing myths*. Coders Kitchen. https://www.coderskitchen.com/top-10-popular-software-testing-myths/

10 qualities that can make you a good tester. (2023, March 19). Software Testing Help. https://www.softwaretestinghelp.com/10-qualities-that-can-make-you-a-good-tester/

The ultimate list of 100 software testing quotes. (2016, January 28). Abstracta Software Testing Services. https://abstracta.us/blog/tools/ultimate-list-100-software-testing-quotes/

Top 10 skills to look for in a QA engineer. (n.d.). Baires Dev. https://www.bairesdev.com/software-development/top-qa-engineer-skills/

Top traits of highly effective software testers. (2019, May 7). 3Pillar Global. https://www.3pillarglobal.com/insights/top-traits-of-highly-effec tive-software-testers/

Tozzi, C. (2016, July 12). *Quality assurance and software testing: A brief history*. Sauce Labs. https://saucelabs.com/resources/blog/quality-assurance-and-software-testing-a-brief-history

Tummala, M. (2022, July 30). *5 Major differences between software testing & quality assurance*. Get Software Service. https://www.getsoftware service.com/differences-between-software-testing-quality-assurance/

TutorialsPoint. (n.d.). *SDLC overview*. https://www.tutorialspoint.com/sdlc/sdlc_overview.htm

Types of software testing. (n.d.). Javatpoint. https://www.javatpoint.com/types-of-software-testing

Types of software testing: Different testing types with details. (2023, February 8). Software Testing Help. https://www.softwaretest inghelp.com/types-of-software-testing/

Warcholinski, M. (n.d.). *How many types of software testing are there?* BrainHub. https://brainhub.eu/library/types-of-software-testing

What are the benefits of software testing? (2022, October 14). Mammoth-AI. https://www.mammoth-ai.com/what-are-the-benefits-of-soft ware-testing/

What is a failover? Definition and related FAQs. (n.d.). Druva. https://www.druva.com/glossary/what-is-a-failover-definition-and-related-faqs

What is API security testing and how does it work? (n.d.). Synopsys. https://www.synopsys.com/glossary/what-is-api-security-testing.html

What is API security testing? (n.d.). Smart Bear. https://smartbear.com/learn/api-testing/security/

What is end to end testing: E2E testing framework with examples. (2023, March 26). Software Testing Help. https://www.guru99.com/end-to-end-testing.html

What is interface testing? Know its types, strategy and tools. (2023, March 23). Software Testing Help. https://www.softwaretestinghelp.com/what-is-interface-testing/

What is localization testing and internationalization testing (simple guide). (2023, March 22). Software Testing Help. https://www.softwaretest inghelp.com/localization-and-internationalization-testing/

What is software compatibility testing? (2023, March 22). Software Testing Help. https://www.softwaretestinghelp.com/software-compatibil ity-testing/

What is software quality assurance (SQA): A guide for beginners. (2023, March 15). Software Testing Help. https://www.softwaretest inghelp.com/software-quality-assurance/

Why do you like testing? We have 12 reasons, see where do you fit. (2023, February 19). Software Testing Help. https://www.softwaretest inghelp.com/why-do-you-like-testing/

Why to choose software testing as a career? (2023). Apponix. https://www.apponix.com/blog/Why-to-choose-software-testing-as-a-career.html

Whyman, A. (n.d.). *The world's first computer bug.* Global App Testing. https://www.globalapptesting.com/blog/the-worlds-first-computer-bug-global-app-testing

Wilk, D. (2020, August 25). *What's the difference between quality assurance and testing in the software industry?* Neoteric. https://neoteric.eu/blog/whats-the-difference-between-quality-assurance-and-testing-in-the-software-industry/

Yasar, K. (n.d.). *What is software testing? Definition, types and importance.* TechTarget. https://www.techtarget.com/whatis/definition/software-testing

Yaseen, M. (2021, August 5). *Some myths and facts of software testing.* Nerd for Tech. https://medium.com/nerd-for-tech/sommyths-and-facts-of-software-testing-9168e3084feb

Zuci Systems. (2022, July 20). *Software security testing: Types, tools & techniques.* Medium. https://medium.com/@zuci_systems/software-security-testing-types-tools-techniques-a12e4c2aeddb

Made in the USA
Middletown, DE
14 September 2023